2011 GREATEST POP & ROCK Hits

★ DELUXE ANNUAL EDITION ★

THE BIGGEST HITS ★ THE GREATEST ARTISTS

CONTENTS

Song	Artist	Page
Airplanes	B.o.B. featuring Hayley Williams of Paramore	2
Animal	Neon Trees	8
Barbra Streisand	Duck Sauce	20
Billionaire	Travie McCoy featuring Bruno Mars	24
Bittersweet	Fantasia	32
Boomerang	Plain White T's	38
Born This Way	Lady Gaga	210
Born to Be Somebody	Justin Bieber	15
Firework	Katy Perry	42
Forget You	Cee Lo Green	48
Grenade	Bruno Mars	60
Haven't Met You Yet	Michael Bublé	66
The High Road	Broken Bells	55
Hold My Hand	Michael Jackson featuring Akon	74
Holiday	Vampire Weekend	86
Hollywood	Michael Bublé	100
If I Die Young	The Band Perry	92
Jar of Hearts	Christina Perri	109
Just the Way You Are	Bruno Mars	116
Like We Used To	Rocket to the Moon	123
Marry Me	Train	130
Misery	Maroon 5	135
Need You Now	Lady Antebellum	148
Not Like the Movies	Katy Perry	142
Nothin' on You	B.o.B.	155
The Only Exception	Paramore	162
Perfect Day	Susan Boyle	170
Rhythm of Love	Plain White T's	176
Rocketeer	Far East Movement featuring Ryan Tedder	184
Smile	Uncle Kracker	204
Temporary Home	Carrie Underwood	190
Wake Up Everybody	John Legend	196
You Haven't Seen the Last of Me	Cher (from *Burlesque*)	218

Produced by
Alfred Music Publishing Co., Inc.
P.O. Box 10003
Van Nuys, CA 91410-0003
alfred.com

Printed in USA.

ISBN-10: 0-7390-7984-0
ISBN-13: 978-0-7390-7984-3

Alfred Cares. Contents printed on 100% recycled paper.

AIRPLANES

Words and Music by
JUSTIN FRANKS, TIM SOMMERS,
JEREMY DUSSOLLIET, BOBBY RAY SIMMONS
and ALEX GRANT

F♯m7
D(9)
A
wish right now, wish right now, wish right now. Can we pre-tend that
air - planes in the night sky are like shoot-ing stars? I could real-ly use a
wish right now, wish right now, wish right now.
Verse (rap):
D2
A5
1. I could use a dream or a genie or a wish
to go back to a place much simpler than this.
2. See additional lyrics

F♯m7
D2
A5
'Cause after all the partyin' and smashin' and crashin',
and all the glitz and the glam and the fashion,
F♯m7
D2
A5
and all the pandemonium and all the madness,
there comes a time where you fade to the blackness.
F♯m7
D2
A5
And when you're staring at that phone in your lap,
and you hoping, but them people never call you back.
F♯m7
D(9)
A
But that's just how the story unfolds,
you get another hand soon after you fold.
(with pedal)

F♯m7
D(9)
A
And when your plans unravel, and they sayin' what would you wish for
if you had one chance?
F♯m7
D(9)
A
So airplane, airplane, sorry I'm late.
I'm on my way, so don't close that gate.
F♯m7
D(9)
A
Can we pre-tend that
If I don't make that, then I'll switch my flight,
and I'll be right back at it by the end of the night.
Chorus:
F♯m7
D(9)
A
air - planes in the night sky are like shoot-ing stars?
I could real-ly use a

F♯m7
D(9)
A
wish right now, wish right now, wish right now. Can we pre-tend that
air - planes in the night sky are like shoot-ing stars? I could real-ly use a
1.
wish right now, wish right now, wish right now.
2.
wish right now.
I could real-ly use a wish right now.
(Lead vocal ad lib.)

Verse 2 (rap):
Somebody take me back to the days
Before this was a job, before I got paid,
Before it ever mattered what I had in my bank.
Yeah, back when I was tryin' to get a tip at Subway,
And back when I was rappin' for the hell of it.
But now-a-days, we rappin' to stay relevant.
I'm guessin' that if we can make some wishes outta airplanes,
Then maybe, yo, maybe I'll go back to the days
Before the politics that we call the rap game,
And back when ain't nobody listened to my mix tape,
And back before I tried to cover up my slang.
But this is for Decatur, what's up, Bobby Ray?
So can I get a wish to end the politics
*And get back to the music that started this sh**?*
So here I stand, and then again I say,
I'm hopin' we can make some wishes outta airplanes.
(To Chorus:)

ANIMAL

Words and Music by
TIM PAGNOTTA, TYLER GLENN,
BRANDEN CAMPBELL, ELAINE DOTY
and CHRISTOPHER ALLEN

C
B♭
We're sick like an - i - mals, we play pre - tend. You're just a can - ni - bal and I'm a - fraid I
C
B♭5
won't get out a - live. No, I won't sleep to - night.
Chorus:
F6
Csus
C
C2
Uh oh, I want some more. Uh oh, what are you wait - ing
B♭maj7
F6
for? Take a bite of my heart to - night. Uh oh, I want some more.

F/A
Am
Dm/A
B♭maj7
Uh oh, what are you wait - ing for?
What are you wait - ing
Csus
C
C2
F
B♭
for? Say good - bye to my heart to - night.
Verse 2:
F
C
2. Here we go a - gain. I feel the chem - i - cals kick - in' in. It's get - ting heav - y and I
mf
B♭
C
B♭
wan - na run and hide. I wan - na run and hide. I

F C

do it ev-'ry time. You're kill-ing me now, and

B♭ C

I won't be de-nied by you, the an - i-mal in-side of you.

𝄋 *Chorus:*

F6 Csus C C2

Uh oh, I want some more. Uh oh, what are you wait - ing

B♭maj7 F6

for? Take a bite of my heart to-night. Uh oh, I want some more.

F/A
Am
Dm/A
B♭maj7
To Coda
Uh oh, what are you wait - ing for? What are you wait - ing
Csus
C
C2
Bridge:
B♭maj7
for? Say good - bye to my heart to - night.
Hush, hush, the world is qui - et.
Whoa,
mf
C
B♭
whoa.
Hush, hush, we both can't fight it. It's us that made this mess. Why
F
C
B♭(9)
Whoa, I won't sleep to - night.
can't you un - der - stand?
f

F6
Csus
C
D5
I won't sleep_ to-night._
F6
Csus
C
B♭
F6
D.S. 𝄋 al Coda
Here we go a - gain.
Here we go a - gain.
Here we go a - gain.
mp
Coda
Csus
C
C2
F6
for?
What are you wait - ing…
(Here we go a - gain.)
Uh oh.

Csus
C
C2
Dm
Uh oh.
(Here we go a - gain.)
(Here we go a - gain.
Bb maj7
F
C2
F6
Uh oh.
Say good - bye to my heart to - night.
Uh oh,
F/A
Am
Dm/A
Bb maj7
I want some more.
Uh oh,
what are you wait - ing for?
Csus
C
C2
F6
What are you wait - ing for?
Say good - bye to my heart to - night.

BORN TO BE SOMEBODY

Words and Music by
DIANE WARREN

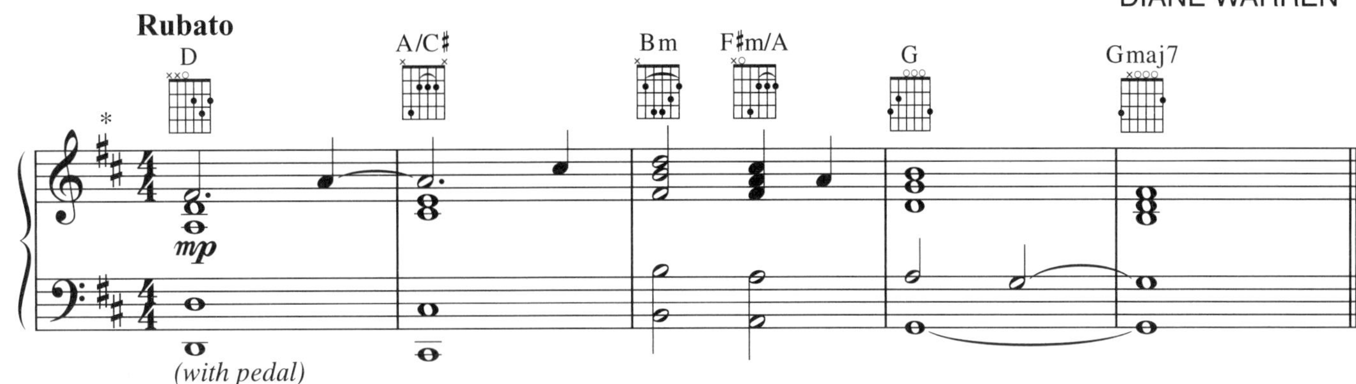

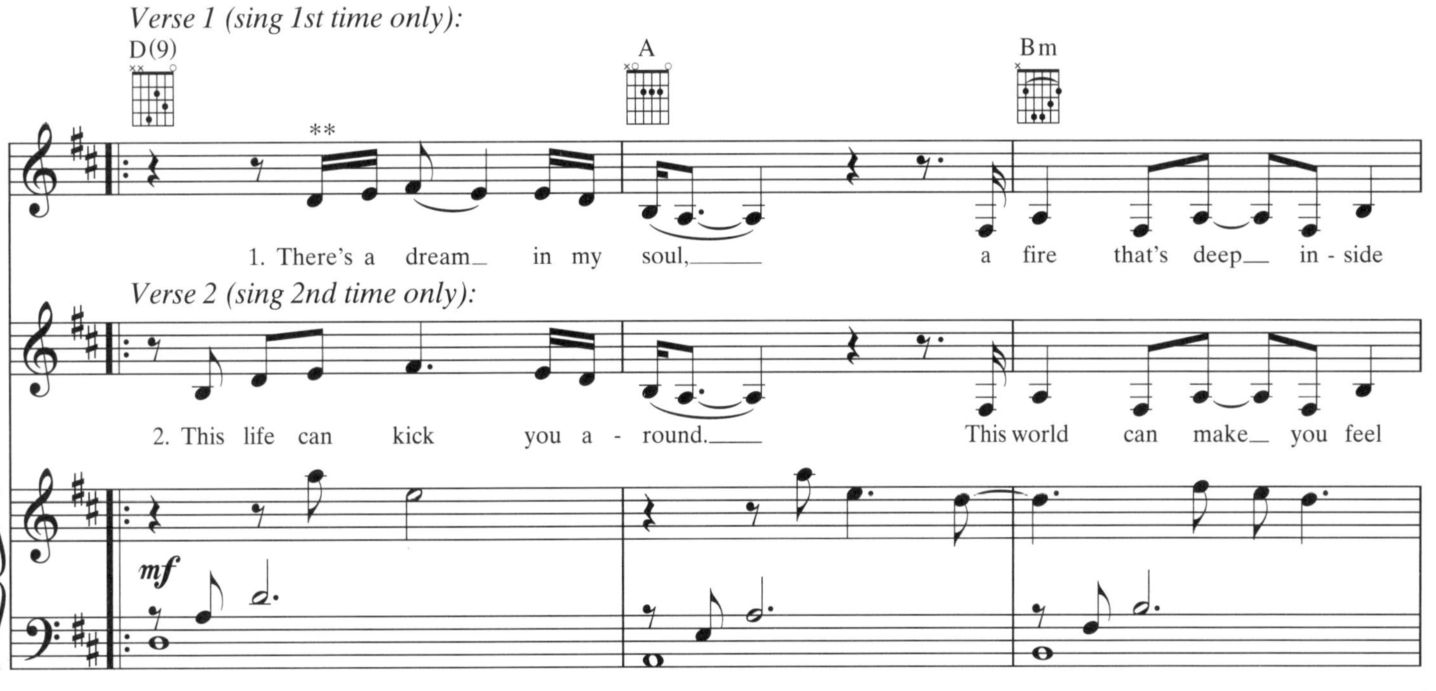

*Recorded in D♭ major.
**Vocals written at pitch.

Bm
Em
wait - ing to be set free.
I'm gon - na see that
I was born to stand tall.
I'm go - ing all the
A/C♯
Bm7
A
G
day.
I can feel it, I can taste it.
way.
I can feel it, I be - lieve it.
E7/G♯
G(9)
Change is com - ing my way.
I was born to be
I'm here, I'm here to stay.
I was born to be

Chorus:
D
A/C♯
some - bod - y. Ain't noth - ing that's ev - er gon - na stop me.
Bm
Asus
G
I'll light up the sky like light - ning. I'm gon - na rise a - bove,
F♯7
G
D
show 'em what I am made of. I was born to be some - bod - y.
A
Em7
1.
G(9)
I was born to be, and this world will be - long to me.

2.
G(9)
Bridge:
Bm7
A
this world will be - long to me.
Feel it, be - lieve it,
N.C.
dream it, be it. I was born to be
cresc.
Chorus:
E
B/D♯
some - bod - y. Ain't noth - ing that's ev - er gon - na stop me.
f
C♯m
G♯m7/B
A
G♯7
I'll light up the sky like light-ning. I'm gon-na rise a-bove, show 'em what I am made of.

A
E
B
F♯m7
I was born to be some-bod-y. I was born to be, and
A(9)
C♯m7
B/D♯
this world will be-long to me.
Oh, oh, oh, oh.
mp
F♯m
E/G♯
A(9)
E
And this world will be-long to me. Yeah,
B/D♯
F♯m
E/G♯
A2
yeah, oh. And this world will be-long to me.
rit.

BARBRA STREISAND

Words and Music by
ALAIN MACKLOVITCH, ARMAND VAN HELDEN,
FRANK FARIAN, FRED JAY,
HEINZ HUTH and JÜERGIN HUTH

E♭
G♭
A♭
Ooh.
Barbra Streisand.
N.C.
1.2.3.

4.
G♭
N.C.
E♭
A♭
4
Bar - bra Strei-sand.
Ooh.
Ooh.
Ooh.
Ooh.

G♭
N.C.
E♭
A♭
4
E♭
Barbra Streisand.
Ooh, ooh, ooh, ooh.
1.
2.
G♭
A♭
G♭
N.C.
E♭
A♭
Barbra Streisand.
Ooh, ooh,
E♭
1.
2.
G♭
A♭
G♭
N.C.
ooh.
Barbra Streisand.

BILLIONAIRE

Words and Music by
PETER HERNANDEZ, PHILIP LAWRENCE,
ARI LEVINE and TRAVIS MCCOY

Moderate reggae feel ♩ = 84

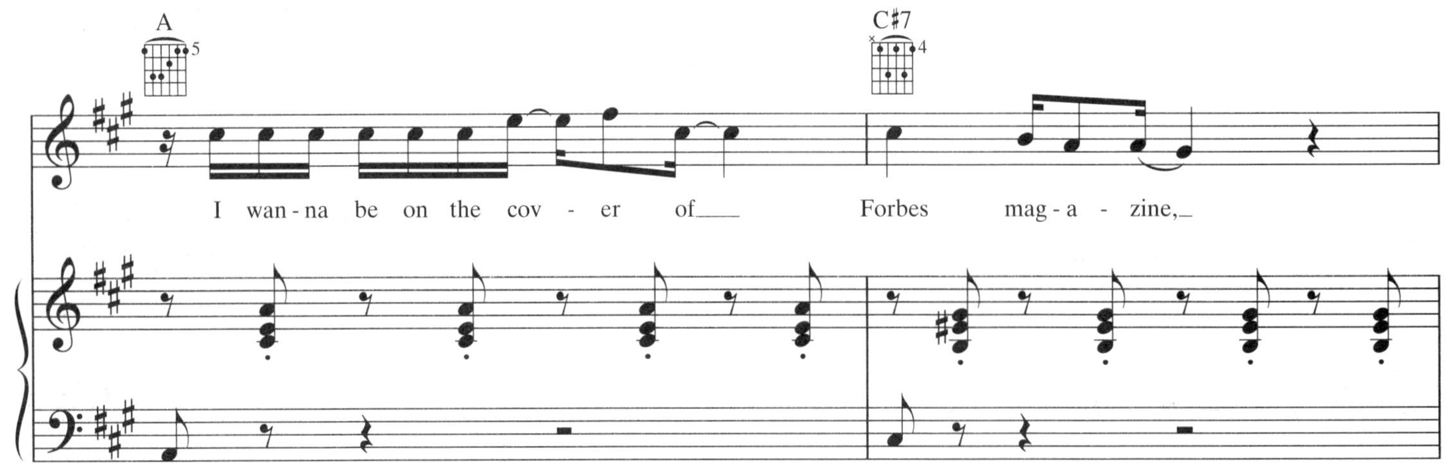

F♯m
E
D
E
smil - ing next to Op - rah and the Queen.
Oh, ev - 'ry time I close my
F♯m
D
E
eyes,
I see my name in shin - ing
F♯m
D
E
lights,
yeah,
a dif - f'rent cit - y ev - 'ry night,
A
A/G♯
F♯m
E
D
oh,
I
swear,
the world bet - ter pre - pare

C♯7
N.C.
for when I'm a bil - lion - aire.
1. (Rap:) Yeah, I would have a
Verse 1:
A
C♯7
show like Oprah. I would be the host of
everyday Christmas. Give Travie a wish list.
mf
F♯m
E
I'd probably pull an Angelina and Brad Pitt, and
adopt a bunch of babies that ain't never had sh**. Give
A
C♯7
away a few Mercedes like, here, lady, have this. And
last, but not least, grant somebody their last wish. It's

F♯m E

been a couple months that I've been single, so you can call me Travie Clause, minus the ho ho.

A C♯7

Get it? I'd probably visit where Katrina hit, and damn sure do a lot more than FEMA did.

F♯m E

Yeah, can't forget about me, stupid. Everywhere I go, I'm-a have my own theme music. Oh,

𝄋 *Bridge:*

D E F♯m

ev - 'ry time I close my eyes, I

D
E
F♯m
see my name in shin - ing lights,
D
E
A
A/G♯
F♯m
E
a dif - f'rent cit - y ev - 'ry night, oh, I
D
C♯7
swear, the world bet - ter pre - pare for when I'm a bil - lion - aire.
F♯m
A
Bm
Oh, oh, when I'm a bil - lion - aire.

F♯m A *To Coda* ⊕ Bm

— Oh, oh. *2. I'll be playing basketball*

Verse 2:

A C♯7

with the President, dunking on his delegates, *then, I'll compliment him on his political etiquette,*

F♯m E

toss a couple milli in the air just for the heck of it, *but keep the fives, twenties, tens, and Bens completely separate.*

A C♯7

Yeah, I'll be in a whole new tax bracket. *We in a recession, but let me take a crack at it.*

F♯m
E
I'll probably take whatever's left and just split it up,
so everybody that I love can have a couple bucks.
A
C♯7
And not a single tummy around me
would know what hunger was, eating good, sleeping soundly.
F♯m
E
I know we all have a similar dream. Go in your pocket,
pull out your wallet, put it in the air and sing.
Chorus:
A
C♯7
I wan-na be a bil-lion-aire
so freak-in' bad,
mp

F♯m
E
buy all of the things I nev - er had.
A
C♯7
I wan-na be on the cov - er of
Forbes mag-a - zine,
F♯m
E
D.S. 𝄋 al Coda
smil - ing next to Op - rah and the Queen.
Oh,
Coda
Bm
A
C♯7
I wan-na be a bil - lion-aire
so freak-ing bad.
mp

BITTERSWEET

Words and Music by
CLAUDE KELLY, CHUCK HARMON
and MICHAEL MENTORE

Csus C Csus C Am7(♭5)

just kept__ your love?__ Yes, I un-der-stand; we did have some good times.

o-ver you as__ I said.__ Oh, deep in-side my heart,__ I made the right de-ci-sion.

A♭maj7 Gm7

On the oth-er hand, got me cry-in' all night.__ It was too

But it's kind-a hard when your mind is think-in', "No."__ Did I

Csus C Csus C A♭maj7/B♭ Am7(♭5)

much for__ my mind.__ So, e-ven though I left you,__ I can't for-get you.__ 'Cause

make a big__ mis-take?__ E-ven though I left you,__ I can't for-get you.__ 'Cause

Chorus:
A♭maj7
Gm7
Fm7
Gm7
when I think a - bout you.
(Bkgrd.) It's bit-ter-sweet, it's bit - ter-sweet.
mf
A♭maj7
Gm7
Csus
C
Csus
C
Guess I'll al - ways love you.
It's bit-ter - sweet, it's bit - ter-sweet.
A♭maj7
Gm7
Fm7
Gm7
When we were to - geth - er, you ain't treat me right. Damn, I real - ly love ya; I ain't gon - na lie. 'Cause
1.
A♭maj7
Gm7
A♭maj7/B♭
when I think a - bout you, it's bit - ter-sweet.

2.

A♭maj7 Gm7 A♭maj7/B♭

when I think a - bout you, whoa, ah, it's bit - ter - sweet.

Verse 3:

Am7(♭5) A♭maj7 Gm7

3. *(Spoken:) See, I don't understand. Like, somebody is gonna get hurt out of this situation, and you just hope it's not you.*

mp

Csus C Csus C Am7(♭5)

At times, part of me wants you, part of me don't.

A♭maj7 Gm7

Part of you is miss - in' you; part of me is gone. Part of me is say - in' that the love is still strong.

Csus C Csus C A♭maj7/B♭ Am7(♭5)
Part of me is let-ting go. So, e-ven though I left you, I can't for-get you. Oh,
Chorus:
A♭maj7 Gm7 Fm7 Gm7
when I think a-bout you, it's bit-ter-sweet.
(Bkgrd.) It's bit-ter-sweet, it's bit-ter-sweet.
mf
A♭maj7 Gm7 Csus C Csus C
Guess I'll al-ways, I'll al-ways love you. You are a part of me.
It's bit-ter-sweet, it's bit-ter-sweet.
A♭maj7 Gm7 Fm7 Gm7
When we were to-geth-er, you ain't treat me right. Then I real-ly love you; I ain't gon-na lie.

A♭maj7
Gm7
A♭maj7/B♭
When I think a - bout you, it's bit - ter-sweet.

Am7(♭5)
A♭maj7
My love, my love, my love, it's bit - ter-sweet.
(Lead vocal ad lib. repeat and fade)

Repeat ad lib. and fade
Gm7
Csus
C
Csus
C
Oh, love.

BOOMERANG

Words and Music by
TOM HIGGENSON and JEREMY SMITH

*Original recording down 1/2 step in B.

Am Em7 Am

and I'm put - ty in your hands. I'm un -
But when you say, "Hel - lo," I can't

Em7 F G

der your spell.
ig - nore you.
You send me spin - ning.

𝄋 *Chorus:*

C G Am

You pull me in close, you throw me a - way. I keep com - ing back

F C G

like a boom - er - ang. You tell me to go, you beg me to stay.

Am
F
C
I keep com - ing back like a boom - er - ang.
'Round, a - round, a -
G
Am
1.
F
C
round and back a - gain, a - round, a-round, a - round and back a - gain.
mp
D7
F
C
2.3.
F
round and back a - gain. A -
C
G
Am
To Coda
F
round, a-round, a - round and back a - gain, a - round, a-round, a - round and back a - gain.

Bridge:
Am
F
Am
Boom, boom, boom, and now my heart is rac - ing. Boom, boom, boom,
F
Am
F
and af - ter you, I'm chas - ing. Boom, boom, boom, you got - ta catch me when I
G
D.S. % al Coda
Coda
F
fall. You send me spin - ning. round and back a - gain.
C
D7
F
C
Dm
C
mp

FIREWORK

Words and Music by
KATY PERRY, MIKKEL ERIKSEN,
TOR ERIK HERMANSEN,
SANDY WILHELM and ESTER DEAN

A♭ G♭

Do you ev - er feel, feel so pa - per - thin,
If you on - ly knew what the fu - ture holds.

Fm D♭(9)

like a house of cards, one blow from cav - ing in?
Af - ter a hur - ri - cane comes a rain - bow.

A♭ *(B♭m) G♭ Fm

Do you ev - er feel al - read - y bur - ied deep? Six feet un - der screams, but
May - be a rea - son why all the doors were closed, so you could o - pen one that

D♭(9) A♭ *(B♭m) G♭

no one seems to hear a thing. Do you know that there's still a chance for you?
leads you to the per - fect road. Like a light - ning bolt, your heart will glow,

*Play B♭m chord 2nd time.

Pre-chorus:
Fm
D♭(9)
A♭
'Cause there's a spark in you.
and when it's time, you'll know.
You just got-ta ig - nite
the light
B♭m7(4)
Fm7
D♭(9)
and let
it shine.
Just own
sim.
A♭
B♭m7(4)
Fm7
the night
like the Fourth
of
Ju - ly.
Chorus:
D♭(9)
A♭
B♭m7(4)
'Cause, ba - by, you're a
fi - re - work.
Come on, show 'em
cresc.

*Sing cue notes 3rd time (on D.S.).

1.
2.
Fm7
D♭(9)
D♭(9)
awe, awe, awe.
Bridge:
Fm7
D♭(9)
Boom, boom, boom, e - ven bright - er than the moon, moon, moon.
A♭
It's al - ways been in - side of you, you, you.
E♭
D.S. 𝄋 al Coda
And now, it's time to let it through. 'Cause, ba - by, you're a

Coda
Fm7
D♭(9)
A♭
4
awe,
awe,
awe.
Boom,
boom,
boom,
B♭m7(4)
4
Fm7
D♭(9)
e - ven bright - er than the moon,
moon,
moon.
A♭
4
B♭m7(4)
4
Boom,
boom,
boom,
e - ven bright - er than the
Fm7
D♭(9)
moon,
moon,
moon.

FORGET YOU

Words and Music by
CHRISTOPHER BROWN, PETER HERNANDEZ,
ARI LEVINE, PHILIP LAWRENCE
and THOMAS "CEE LO" CALLAWAY

F
C
wasn't enough. I'm like, for-get you and for-get her too. Said if
D
F
C
I was rich-er, I'd still be wit' ya.
Ha, now ain't that some sh?
D
(Ain't that some sh?) And al-though there's pain in my chest, I still
F
C
wish you the best with a for-get you.
1. Yeah, I'm

Verse:
D
F
sor - ry I can't af - ford a Fer - ra - ri, but
I know that I had to bor - row,
C
that don't mean I can't get you there.
beg and steal and lie and cheat,
I guess he's an
try - in' to
D
F
X - box and I'm more an A - tar - i, but the
keep ya, try - in' to please ya, 'cause
C
way you play your game ain't fair.
be - ing in love with your a** ain't cheap.
I pit - y the fool

D
F
C
that falls in love with you, oh, oh. (Oh, sh, she's a gold - dig-ger.) Well.
(Just thought you should know it.) Ooh, I've
got some news for you, ha ha.
(Spoken:) Yeah, go and run and tell your little boyfriend.
(Spoken:) Ooh, I really hate your a** right now.
See you
Chorus:
driv - in' 'round town with the girl I love, and I'm like, for - get you.

D
F
I guess the change in my pock - et wasn't e - nough. I'm like,
C
D
for - get you and for - get her too. Said if I was rich - er, I'd
F
C
still he wit' ya. Ha, now ain't that some sh?
D
(Ain't that some sh?) And al - though there's pain in my chest, I still

To Coda
1.
F
C
wish you the best with a for - get you.
2. Now,
2.
Bridge:
Em
Am
Now, ba - by, ba - by, ba - by, why you wan - na, wan - na hurt me so bad?
Dm7
Fmaj7/G
Em
E
(So bad, so bad, so bad.) I tried to tell my ma - ma, but she
Am
G/B
Am/C
A7/C♯
D7
told me, "This is one for your dad."
Yes, she
(Your dad, your dad,

Fmaj7/G
D7
N.C.
F
N.C.
did.
your dad.
And I'm like,
why,
why,
(Uh,
uh,
Fmaj7/G
Am
G/B
Am/C
A7/C♯
D7
N.C.
why,
la - dy?
I love you,
uh.)
F
N.C.
G
D.S. 𝄋 al Coda
N.C.
I still love you.
Oh,
I see you
𝄌 Coda
Uh.

THE HIGH ROAD

Words and Music by
JAMES MERCER and BRIAN BURTON

Moderate hip-hop beat ♩ = 80

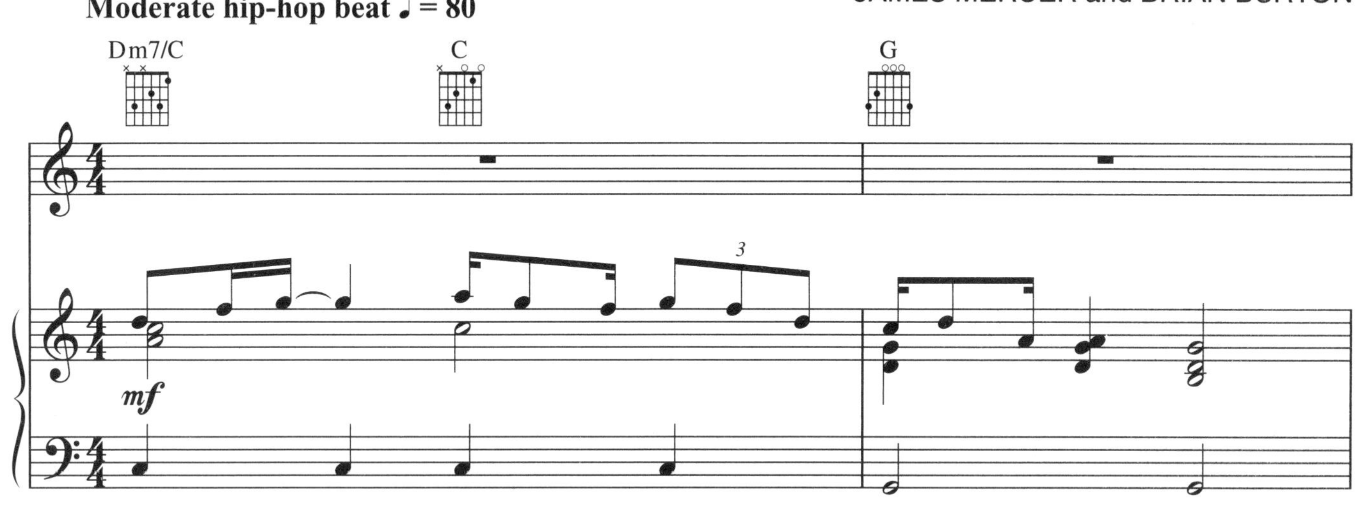

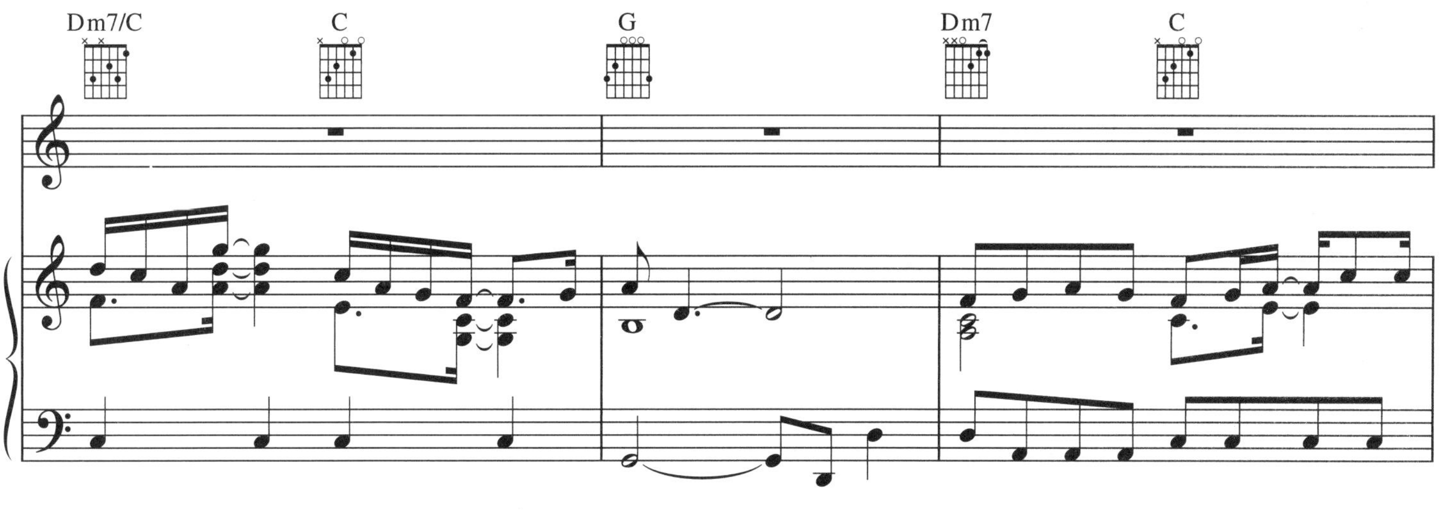

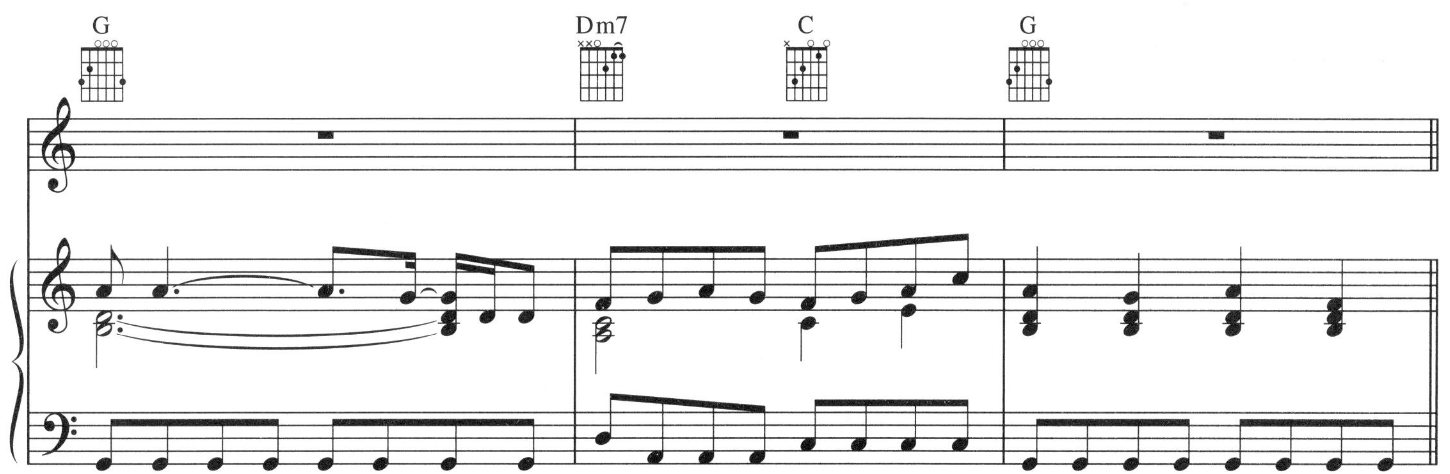

Verse:
Dm
C
Dm
C
1. We're down_ to wait_ all night._ She's bound_ to run_ a - mok._
2. The dawn_ to end_ all nights;_ that's all_ we hoped_ it was,_
Dm
C
G
In - vest - ed e - nough_ in it an - y - how._ To each_ his own._
a break_ from the war - fare in_ your house._ To each_ his own._
Dm
C
Dm
C
The gar - den needs sort - ing out._ She curls_ her lips on the bow,_
The sol - dier is bail - ing out_ and curled_ his lips on the bow,_
Dm
C
G
and I_ don't know_ if I'm dead_ or not,_ to an - y - one._
and I_ don't know_ if the dead_ can talk_ to an - y - one._

Dm
C
Dm
C
Come on and get the min - i - mum before you o - pen up your eyes.
Come on and get the min - i - mum before you o - pen up your eyes.
Dm
C
G
This ar - my has so man - y hands to an - a - lyze.
This ar - my has so man - y hands. Are you one of us?
Dm
C
Dm
C
Come on and get your o - ver - dose. Col - lect it at the bor - der - line.
Come on and get your o - ver - dose. Col - lect it at the bor - der - line.
Dm
C
G
And they want to get up in your head.
And they want to get up in your head.
'Cause they

Chorus:
Dm
C
G
know and so do I
the high
road is hard to find;
a de-
tour in your new life.
Tell all
of your friends good - bye.
1.

2.
Bridge:
G
F
G
Dm
F
G
Am
G
It's
C
C/E
F
C/E
too late to change your mind.
You let loss
Dm
1.2.3.
G7
4.
G7
be your guide.
It's

GRENADE

Words and Music by
CLAUDE KELLY, PETER HERNANDEZ,
BRODY BROWN, PHILIP LAWRENCE,
ARI LEVINE and ANDREW WYATT

Am

__ it in the trash, _ you tossed __ it in the trash, _ you did. ____ To give_

Dm Bb

__ me all your love __ is all ____ I ev - er asked. _ 'Cause what you don't un - der - stand_

A7 N.C.

__ is I'd catch a gre - nade ____

Chorus:

Dm Bb F C

for you, throw my hand on a blade_
(Yeah, yeah, yeah. _)

mf

Dm Bb F C Dm Bb

__ for you. I'd jump in front of a train __ for you.
(Yeah, yeah, yeah. _) (Yeah,

F
C
Dm
B♭
F
C
You know I'd do an - y - thing for you.
Oh, I would
yeah, yeah.)
(Yeah, yeah, yeah.)
B♭
C
F
A7
go through all this pain, take a bul - let straight through my brain.
Dm
C
B♭
1.
A
N.C.
Yes, I would die for you, ba - by, but you won't do the same.
Dm
Am
No, no, no.

2.

Bridge:

A N.C. Gm

but you won't do the same. If my

Dm

bod - y was on fi - re, ooh, you'd watch me burn down in flames.

Gm A7

You said you loved me. You're a li - ar, 'cause you nev - er, ev - er,

Dm

ev - er___ did, ba - by.

mp

B♭
A7
N.C.
Dm
B♭
But, dar - ling, I'd still catch a gre - nade for you,
mf
F
C
Dm
B♭
F
C
throw my hand on a blade for you.
I'd jump in front of a train
Dm
B♭
F
C
Dm
B♭
for you.
You know I'd do an - y - thing for you.
F
C
B♭
C
Oh, I would go through all this pain,

F
A7
Dm
C
B♭
take a bul-let straight through my brain.
Yes, I would die for you, ba - by,
A7
N.C.
Dm
but you won't do the same.
No, you won't do the same.
mp
Am
Dm
You would-n't do the same,
ooh,
Am
N.C.
you nev-er do the same,
no, no, no, no.

HAVEN'T MET YOU YET

Words and Music by
MICHAEL BUBLÉ, ALAN CHANG
and AMY FOSTER

G♭maj7
E♭m9
B♭m7
A♭
prised, not ev - 'ry-thing lasts. I've bro - ken my heart so man - y times, I've stopped
wait. I'll nev - er give up. I guess it's half tim - ing and the oth - er half's
D♭
G♭maj7
E♭m9
keep-ing track. Talk my - self in, I talk my - self out, I get all worked up,
luck. Wher - ev-er you are, when-ev - er it's right, you'll come out of no -
A♭
B♭/D
E♭m7
D♭/F
then I let my - self down. I tried so ver - y hard not to lose it.
where and in - to my life. And I know that we can be so a - maz - ing.
E♭m7
A♭
E♭m7
I came up with a mil - li - on ex - cus - es. I thought I thought of
And, ba - by, your love is gon - na change me. And now I can see

D♭/F
G♭
A♭
ev - 'ry___ pos - si - bil - i - ty.
And I know some - day___
ev - 'ry___ pos - si - bil - i - ty.
And some - how, I know_
Chorus:
G♭maj7
A♭
D♭
G♭maj7
A♭
that it - 'll all___ turn out.
You'll make me work___ so we can work_ to work it out._
B♭m
E♭m7
F7
B♭m7
D♭7
And I prom - ise you, kid,___ that I'll give___ so much more_ than I get.
G♭
1.
A♭
D♭
G♭maj7
I just have - n't met you yet.
Mm.

E♭m9
B♭m7
A♭
2.
A♭
just have - n't met you
Bridge:
B♭m
F/A
D♭7/A♭
yet. They say all's fair in
E♭7/G
E♭m7
D♭/F
love and war. But I won't need to fight it. We'll
G♭
A♭
get it right and we'll be u - nit - ed.

A♭maj7
B♭
E♭
A♭maj7
B♭
Cm
f
A♭maj7
G7
Cm7
E♭7
A♭
B♭
Fm7
E♭/G
Fm7
And I know that we can be so a - maz - ing.
And be - ing in your
mf
B♭
Fm7
E♭/G
life is gon - na change me.
And now I can see ev - 'ry sin - gle pos -

A♭
B♭
si - bil - i - ty,
mm.
And some-day I know
Chorus:
A♭maj7
B♭
E♭
A♭maj7
B♭
it - 'll all turn out.
And I'll work to work
mp
Cm
Fm7
G7
Cm7
E♭7
it out.
Prom - ise you, kid,
I'll give more than
A♭
B♭
I get, than I get, than I get, than I get.
Oh, you know
cresc. poco a poco

A♭maj7
B♭
E♭
A♭maj7
B♭
it - 'll all turn out.
And you'll make me work so we can work to work it out.
Cm
Fm7
G7
Cm7
E♭7
And I prom - ise you, kid, to give so much more than I get.
A♭
B♭
E♭
Yeah, I just have - n't met you yet.
A♭maj7
Fm9
Cm7
B♭
I just have - n't met you

E♭
A♭maj7
Fm9
yet. Oh, I prom - ise you, kid, to give so much more than I get.
Cm7
B♭
E♭
A♭maj7
(I said, love, love, love, love,
Fm9
Cm7
B♭
E♭
love, love, love, love, love, love,
I just have - n't met you yet.
A♭maj7
Fm9
Cm7
B♭
E♭
love, love, love, love.) I just have - n't met you yet.

HOLD MY HAND

Words and Music by
CLAUDE KELLY, AKON and GIORGIO TUINFORT

*Recorded in D♭ major.

C G Am F

so tell me what_ we're wait - ing for?

Hold my hand.

C G Am F

We're bet-ter off_ be - ing_ to - geth - er

Hold my hand.

C G Am F

than be-ing mis - 'ra - ble_ a - lone. 'Cause

Hold my hand.

C
G
Am
F
I've been there be-fore and you've been there be-fore, but to-geth-er, we can be al - right. 'Cause
when it gets dark and when it gets cold, we hold each oth-er 'til we see the sun - light. So if you just
Chorus:
hold my hand, ba - by, I'll prom - ise that I'll do
Bkgrd. vocals:
Hold my hand.

C
G
Am
F
all
I
can,
things will go bet - ter if you just
All
I
can.
C
G
Am
F
hold
my
hand.
Noth-ing can come be - tween us if you just
Hold
my
hand.
C
G
Am
F
hold my,
hold my,
hold my hand.
Hold my hand.
Hold my,
hold my,
hold my hand.

Verse 2:
C
G
Am
F
2. The night's_are get - ting dark - er,
Hold my hand.
C
G
Am
F
and there's_no peace in - side.
Hold my hand.
C
G
Am
F
So why make our lives hard - er,
yeah,
Hold my hand.

C
G
Am
F
by fight - ing love to - night. 'Cause
Ba - by.
So...
I've been there be - fore and you've been there be - fore, but to - geth - er, we can be al - right. 'Cause
Al - right,
when it gets dark and when it gets cold, we hold each oth - er 'til we see the sun - light. So if you just
'til we see the sun - light.

Chorus:
C G Am F
hold my hand, ba - by, I'll prom - ise that I'll do
Hold my hand.
C G Am F
all I can, things will go bet - ter if you just
All I can.
C G Am F
hold my hand. Noth-ing can come be - tween us if you just
Hold my hand.

C
G
Am
F
hold my, hold my, hold my hand. Hold my hand.
Hold my, hold my, hold my hand.
Verse 3:
3. I could tell that you're tired of be-ing lone - ly. Take my hand, don't let go, ba-by, hold me.
Yeah.
Hold my
Come to me and let me be your one and on - ly. 'Cause I could make it al - right 'til the morn - ing.
hand. Hold my hand. Hold my

C
G
Am
F
I could tell that you're tired of be-ing lone - ly.
Take my hand, don't let go, ba-by, hold me.
hand.
Hold my hand.
Ooh.
C
G
Am
F
Come to me and let me be your one and on - ly.
'Cause I could make it al - right 'til the morn - ing.
One and on - ly.
Hold my
Chorus:
C
G
Am
F
Hold my hand, ba - by, I'll prom - ise that I'll do
Hold my hand.
hand.

C
G
Am
F
all I can, things will go bet - ter if you just
All I can.
C
G
Am
F
hold my hand.
Noth-ing can come be - tween us if you just
Hold my hand.
C
G
Am
F
hold my, hold my, hold my hand. Hold my
Hold my, hold my, hold my hand.

C
G
Am
F
hand.
Hold my hand.
Yeah,
yeah.
Hold my hand.
C
G
Am
F
All I can.
Hold my hand.
All I can.
C
G
Am
F
Hold my hand.
Noth-ing can come be - tween us if you just...
Hold my hand.

C
G
Am
F
Whoo! Whoo! Whoo! Whoo! Hold my
Hold my, hold my, hold my hand.
C
G
Am
F
hand.
Mm.
3
C
G
Am
F
C
(Whispered:) Hold my hand.
rall.

HOLIDAY

Lyrics by
EZRA KOENIG

Music by
CHRIS BAIO, ROSTAM BATMANGLIJ,
EZRA KOENIG and CHRISTOPHER TOMSON

Fast ♩ = 154

D

mf

𝄋 *Verses 1 & 3:*

G(9) D A
neath my sheets_ while I cov - er both__ my ears.____ But
gas - o - line,__ but the oth - er half's__ the surf.____ So
Chorus:
G A7/C♯ D G A7/C♯
if I wait__ for a hol - i - day,__ could it stop__ my fear?_
D A7/C♯ D G
__ To go a - way__ on a sum-mer's day__
A7/C♯ To Coda D
nev - er seemed_ so clear.___

Verse 2:
D
2. Holiday still so far away, our republic on the beach. I
G(9)
D
A/C♯
D
can't forget just how bad it gets when I'm counting on my teeth.
G(9)
D/F♯
A/E
Chorus:
G
A7/C♯
D
G
But if I wait for a holiday,

A7/C♯
D
G
A7/C♯
could it stop my fear?
To go a-way on a
D
G
A7/C♯
D
sum-mer's day
nev-er seemed so clear.
N.C.

Bridge:
G
A7/C♯
D
A veg - e - tar - i - an since___ the in - va - sion, she'd nev - er seen__ the word
G
A7/C♯
bombs. She'd nev - er seen__ the word bombs blown_ up to
D
G
nine - ty - six point__ Fu - tur - a. She'd nev - er seen__ an A
A7/C♯
D
G
K in a yel - low - y Day - Glo dis - play. A

A7/C♯

T - shirt so love - ly it turned___ all the his - t'ry books

D

grey.

D.S. 𝄋 al Coda

𝄌 Coda

D

IF I DIE YOUNG

Words and Music by
KIMBERLY PERRY

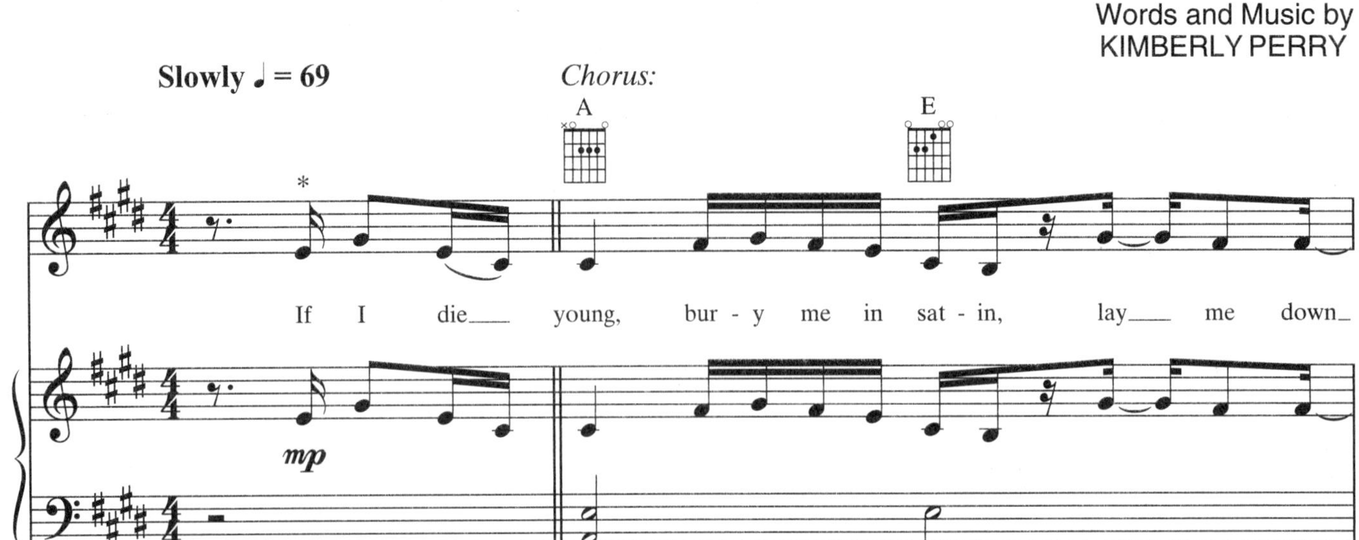

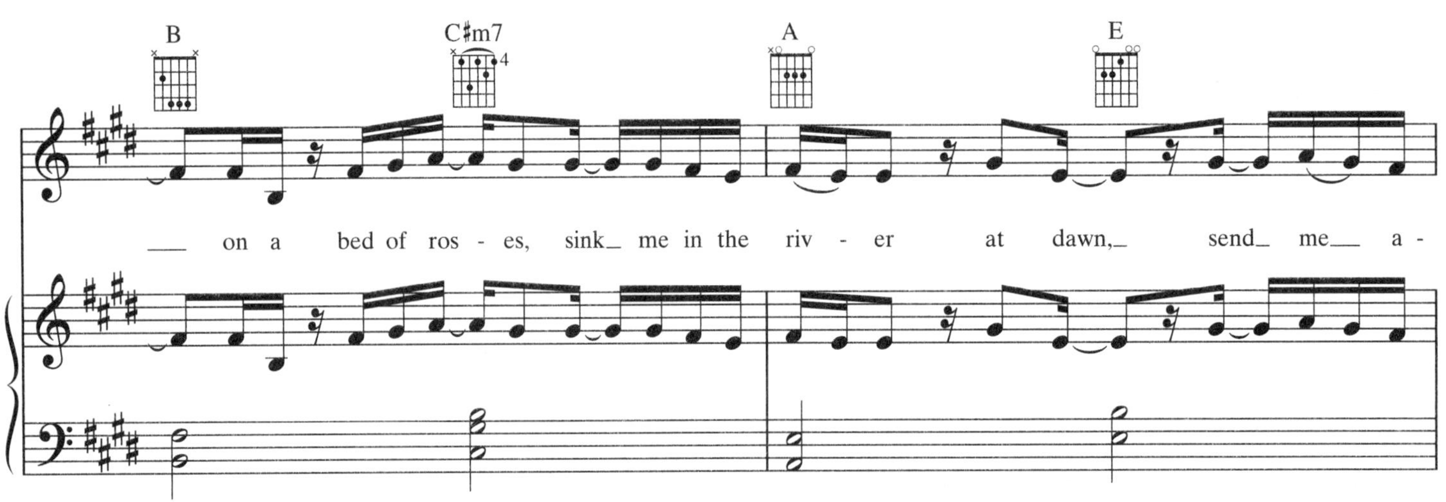

*All vocals written at pitch.

Verse 1:
B E/B B7 A E
1. Lord, make me a rain - bow, I'll shine down on my moth-er. She'll know I'm safe with
mf
B C#m7 A E
you when she stands un-der my col-ors. Oh, and life ain't al-ways what you think it ought to be, no,
B C#m7 A E
ain't e-ven gray, but she bur-ies her ba - by. The sharp knife of a short life.
B C#m7 A E
Well, I've had just e-nough time.

Chorus:
B
E/B
B7
A
E
If I die young, bur-y me in sat-in, lay me down
B
C♯m7
A
E
on a bed of ros-es, sink me in the riv-er at dawn, send me a-
B
C♯m7
A
E
way with the words of a love song. The sharp knife of a short life.
B
C♯m7
A
E
Well, I've had just e-nough

Verse 2:
B
E/B
B7
A
E
time.
2. And I'll be wear-ing white
when I come_ in-to your king-dom. I'm as
B
C♯m7
A
E
green as the ring on my lit-tle cold fin-ger. I've
nev-er known_ the lov - ing of a man, but it
B
C♯m7
A
E
sure felt nice when he was hold-ing my hand. There's a
boy here in town, says he'll love me for-ev-er.
B
C♯m7
A
E
Who would have thought for-ev - er could be sev-ered by___ the sharp_ knife of a short_ life._

B
C♯m7
A
E
Well, I've had just e - nough time.
E/B
B7
Bridge:
So put on your best boys and I'll wear my pearls.
mp
rit.

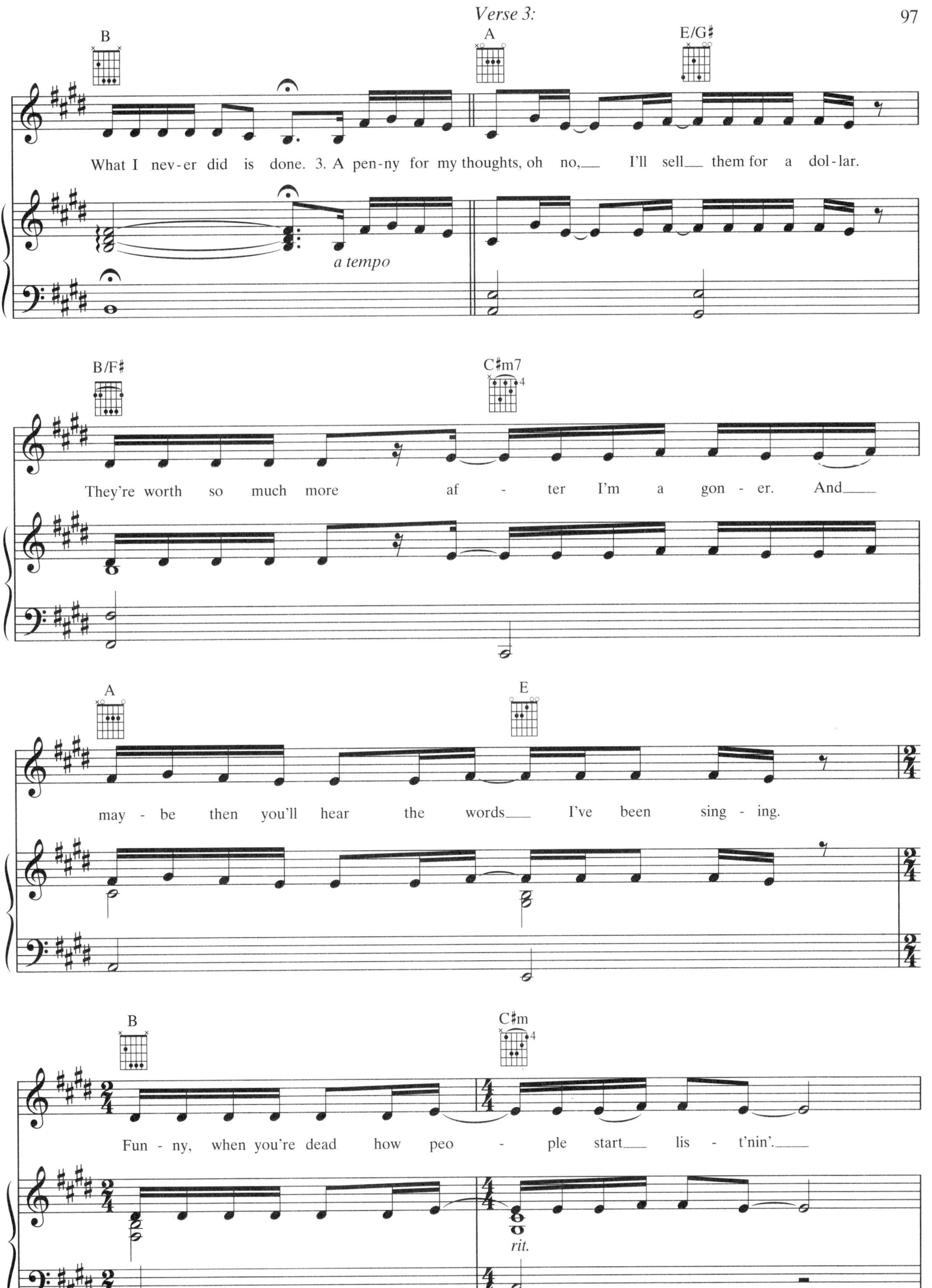
Verse 3:
B
A
E/G♯
What I nev-er did is done. 3. A pen-ny for my thoughts, oh no,___ I'll sell___ them for a dol-lar.
a tempo
B/F♯
C♯m7
They're worth so much more af - ter I'm a gon - er. And___
A
E
may - be then you'll hear the words___ I've been sing - ing.
B
C♯m
Fun - ny, when you're dead how peo - ple start___ lis - t'nin'.___
rit.

A
E
B
E/B
B7
If I die
a tempo
Chorus:
C♯m7
young, bur - y me in sat - in, lay me down on a bed of ros - es, sink me in the
mf
riv - er at dawn, send me a - way with the words of a love song. Uh
oh, the bal - lad of the dove. Go with peace and love.
(Uh oh, uh oh.)

A
E
B
C♯m7
Gath-er up your tears, keep_ 'em in your pock-et. Save them for a time when you're real-ly gon-na need them. Oh,_
A
E
B
C♯m7
_ the sharp_ knife of a short_ life. Well,
A
E
B
E/B
B7
I've had just e-nough time. So
rit.
Freely
A
E
N.C.
put on your best boys and I'll wear my pearls.
mp
rit.

HOLLYWOOD

Words and Music by
MICHAEL BUBLÉ and ROBERT G. SCOTT

F7
Fm7
C
on my T V, will you smile and wave at me, tell - ing O - prah who you are?
flush your cav - i - ar and your mil - lion dol - lar car, I don't need that kind of girl.
So you want to be a rock star,
with blue - eyed bun - nies in your
But could you be the next sen - sa - tion,
or will you set the lat - est
(Play cue notes 2nd time)
D7
F7
bed? Mmm.
Well, re - mem - ber when you're rich that you
style?
You don't need a catch - y song 'cause the

Fm7
C
sold your-self for this, you'll be fa - mous 'cause you're dead.
So don't go high -
kids - 'll sing a - long when you sell it with a smile.
Chorus:
Em7
Am7
F
er for de - si -
mf
C
C/B
Am
Am/G
D7/F♯
Fm7
re. Put it in your head, ba - by, Hol - ly - wood is dead, you can find it in your -
1.
C
N.C.
self. 2. I don't want to take you
2.
C
F/C
C
self.

F/C C Em7 Am7
So don't fly high - er for your fi -
F C C/B Am Am/G
re. Put it in your head, ba - by, Hol - ly - wood is
D7/F♯ Fm7 C F/C C F/C C
dead, you can find it in your - self.
Interlude:
F Fm
f
Na, na, na - na - na - na. Keep it in your head, Hol - ly - wood is dead.

Verse 3:
C
N.C.
C
3. Well, you can do the mon - ey tan - go,
D7
or you can start your lit - tle band.
You can swing
F
Fm
C
from vine to vine while the cut - ies wait in line with the mon - ey in their hands.
But if you get to Cal - i - for - nia,
save a piece of gold

D7
F
for me.
And it's the only thing you'll save, but I'll
Fm
C
bet you'll nev - er wave when I watch you on T V.
So don't go high -
Chorus:
Em7
Am7
F
er for de - si -
C
C/B
Am
Am/G
D7/F♯
Fm7
re. Put it in your head, ba - by, Hol - ly - wood is dead, you can find it in your -

C
Em7
self.
So don't fly high
-
Am7
F
C
C/B
er
for your
fi
-
re.
Put it in your
Am
Am/G
D7/F♯
Fm7
C
head, ba - by, Hol - ly-wood is dead, you can find it in your - self.
C
C/B
Am
Am/G
D7/F♯
Fm7
Keep on lov - in' what is true and the world will come to you, you can find it in your-

C
C/B
Am
Am/G
self.
Love what is true and the world will come to
D7/F#
Fm7
C
you, you can find it in your - self.
No, no, no, no,
F
Fm
no,
keep it in your head,
Hol - ly - wood is dead.
Na, na, na - na - na - na,
na, na - na - na - na,
na, na - na - na - na.
C
Gm
/F
No, no, Hol - ly - wood is dead, babe.
ff

/E♭
/D
E♭
Gm/D
G
Oh,
F
Hol - ly - wood is dead, dead.
Ooo, it's dead,
Na, na, na - na - na - na,
na, na - na - na - na,
f
Fm
C
Repeat ad lib. and fade
Hol - ly - wood is dead, babe, babe, ba - by, babe, no, no, no, no, no, no.
na, na - na - na - na.

JAR OF HEARTS

Words and Music by
DREW LAWRENCE, CHRISTINA PERRI
and BARRETT YERETSIAN

Fm
A♭
Cm
B♭
Fm
A♭
I learned to live half a-live, and now you want me one more
B♭sus
B♭
Chorus:
E♭
B♭
time.
And who do you think you are?
Run-ning 'round leav-ing
Cm
A♭
A♭m
scars, col-lect-ing your jar of hearts, and tear-ing love a-part.
E♭
B♭
You're gon-na catch a cold from the ice in-side your

Cm
Ab
Abm
Eb
Bb/D
soul, so don't come back for me. Who do you think you are?
Verse 2:
Cm
Eb
Bb
2. I hear you're ask - ing all a - round if I am an - y - where to be
Fm
Cm
Eb
found. But I have grown too strong
Bb
Ab
Eb/G
Fm
Ab
to ev - er fall back in your arms. And I learned to live

Cm
B♭
Fm
A♭
B♭sus
B♭
half a - live,
and now you want me one more time.
Chorus:
E♭
B♭
And who do you think you are?
Run - ning 'round leav - ing
Cm
A♭
A♭m
scars,
col - lect - ing your jar of hearts,
and tear - ing love a - part.
E♭
B♭
You're gon - na catch a cold
from the ice in - side your

Cm
To Coda
A♭
A♭m
E♭
soul, so don't come back for me. Who do you think you are? And
Bridge:
Cm
G/B
Cm7/B♭
F/A
Cm
G/B
it took so long just to feel al - right, re - mem - ber how to put back the
Cm7/B♭
F/A
Cm
G/B
Cm7/B♭
F/A
light in my eyes. I wish I had missed the first time that we kissed 'cause
Cm
G/B
Cm7/B♭
F/A
you broke all your prom - is - es. And

A♭
G
D.S. 𝄋 al Coda
now you're back, you don't get to get me back.
𝄌 Coda
A♭
A♭m
E♭
me. Don't come back at all. And who do you think you are?
B♭
Cm
Run-ning 'round leav - ing scars, col - lect - ing your jar of hearts,
A♭
A♭m
E♭
and tear - ing love a - part. You're gon - na catch a cold

B♭
Cm
from the ice in - side your soul.
Don't come back for
A♭
A♭m
E♭
me.
Don't come back at all.
A♭dim7
E♭
A♭dim7
Who do you think you are?
Who do you think you
E♭
A♭dim7
E♭
are?
Who do you think you are?
rall.

JUST THE WAY YOU ARE

Words and Music by
KHALIL WALTON, PETE HERNANDEZ,
PHIL LAWRENCE, ARI LEVINE
and KHARI CAIN

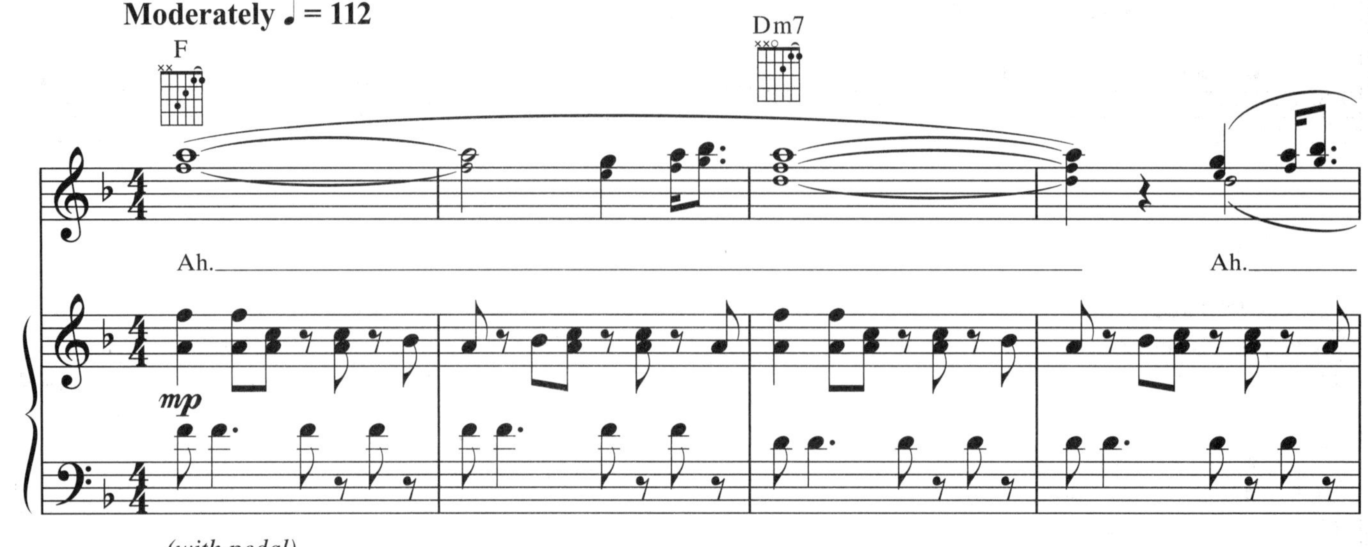

B♭maj9
perfect-ly with-out her try-ing. She's so beau-ti-ful, and I tell her ev-'ry
F
day. Yeah, I know, I know when I
mf
Dm7
com-pli-ment her, she won't be-lieve me. And it's so, it's so sad to think that she don't see what I see.
B♭maj9
F
But ev-'ry time she asks me, "Do I look o-kay?" I say…

Chorus:
When I see your face,
there's not a thing
that I would change,
'cause your a - maz - ing,
just
the way you are.
And when you smile,
the whole world stops and stares for a while,
Dm7
B♭maj9
F
Dm7
f

B♭maj9

— 'cause, girl, you're a - maz - ing, just — the way — you are. —

F

To Coda ⊕

— Yeah. —

Verse 2:

2. Her lips, — her lips, — I could

mf

Dm7

kiss them all — day if — she'd let me. Her laugh, — her laugh — she hates, but I — think it's — so sex - y.

B♭maj9

F

She's so beau - ti - ful, — and I tell her ev - 'ry — day. —

Oh, you know, you know, you know I'd nev - er ask you to change._ If
Dm7
B♭maj9
per-fect's what you're search-ing for, then just stay the same._ So,___ don't e-ven both - er ask - ing if_
F
D.S. 𝄋 al Coda
___ you look_ o - kay._ You know I'll say...___ When I see your face,_
𝄌 Coda
The way_ you are,___ the way_ you are,_

Dm7
B♭maj9
girl, you're a - maz - ing, just
F
the way you are.
When I see your face,
Chorus:
Dm7
mp
there's not a thing that I would change,
B♭maj9
'cause your a - maz - ing, just the way you are.

F
And when you smile,
mf
Dm7
the whole world stops and stares for a while,
B♭maj9
'cause, girl, you're a - maz - ing,
just
F
the way you are.
Yeah.

LIKE WE USED TO

Words and Music by
NICK SANTINO, JUSTIN RICHARDS,
ERIC HALVORSEN, ANDREW COOK,
DAN YOUNG and LOREN BRINTON

Moderately slow ♩ = 88

D D/F♯ G(9) D Asus

Whoa.

mp

(with pedal)

D D/F♯ G(9)

Verse 1 (sing 1st time only):

D D/F♯ G(9)

1. I can feel her breath as she's sleep - ing next_ to me,_

Verse 2 (sing 2nd time only):

2. Four-teen months_ and sev - en days_ a - go,_ oh, I know you know_

mf

Bm7
Asus
G(9)
shar - ing pil - lows and cold feet.
how we felt a - bout that night.
D
D/F♯
G(9)
She can feel my heart, fell a - sleep to its beat,
Just your skin a - gainst the win - dow, oh, we took it slow,
Bm7
Asus
G(9)
un - der blank - ets and warm sheets.
and we both know

Em
D
A
Asus
A
If on - ly I could be in that bed a - gain.
it should have been me in - side that car.
Em
D
A
N.C.
If on - ly it were me in - stead of him.
Does he watch
It should have been me in - stead of him in the dark.
Does he watch
Chorus:
D
D/F♯
your fa - v'rite mov - ies? Does he hold you when you cry? Does he let you
f

G(9)
Bm
A
3
tell him all___ your fa - v'rite parts_ when you've seen it a mil-lion times?_ Does he sing_
D
Em7
___ to all___ your mu - sic while you dance___ to Pur - ple Rain?_ Does he do
Bm
A
G(9)
1.
D
D/F♯
all_____ these things like I used_ to?_____
mf
G(9)
D
Asus
D
D/F♯
G(9)
Bm/D
Asus

2.

Bridge:

D G

I know love

Well, I'm a

D Em D/F♯ Asus

hap-pens all the time, love.

You're on my

suck-er for that feel-ing.

I al-ways end up feel-ing cheat-ed.

G

mind, love,

and that hap-pens all the

Oh, dar-ling, I know I'm not need-ed.

D Em D/F♯ A Asus A
time, love, yeah. Will he love
Chorus:
D D/F♯
you like I loved you? Will he tell you ev - 'ry day? Will he make you
G(9) Bm A
feel that you're in - vin - ci - ble with ev - 'ry word he'll say? Can you prom-
D Em7
ise me if this one's right, don't throw it all a - way? Can you do

Bm
A
G
all these things,
will you do all these
G
N.C.
D
D/F♯
things like we used to,
mp
G(9)
D
Asus
oh, like we used to?
rit.

MARRY ME

Words and Music by
SAM HOLLANDER
and PAT MONAHAN

Moderately 𝅗𝅥 = 88

C/E F2

mp

(with pedal)

C/E F2

Verse:

C Gsus/B G/B

1. For - ev - er could nev - er be long e - nough_ for me to
2. To - geth - er can nev - er be close e - nough_ for me to

Am7 Gsus F2

feel like I've had long e - nough_ with you.
feel like I am close e - nough_ to you.

C
Gsus/B
G/B
For - get the world, now, we won't let them see.
You wear white and I'll wear out the words "I love
Am7
Gsus
F2
But there's one thing left to do.
you" and "you're beau-ti - ful."
C/E
F2
Now that the weight has lift - ed
Now that the wait is o - ver
C/E
F2
and love has sure - ly shift - ed my way,
and love has fi - n'lly showed her my way,

Chorus:
C
Gsus/B
G/B
Am7
mar - ry me to-day
Gsus
F2
C
and ev - 'ry day.
Mar - ry
Gsus/B
G/B
Am7
Gsus
F2
me.
If I ev - er get the nerve to say "hel - lo" in this ca -
C/E
F2
fé, say you will.
Mm,
say you will,

C/E
To Coda
F2
1.
2.
mm.
Bridge:
B♭2
F(9)/A
Prom - ise me you'll al - ways be
C
Gsus/B
G/B
hap - py by my side.
B♭2
F(9)/A
I prom - ise to sing to you

C
Gsus/B
G/B
when all the mu - sic dies.
B♭2
F(9)/A
D.S. 𝄋 al Coda
And
𝄌 Coda
F2
mm,
mar - ry
C/E
F2
me,
mm.

MISERY

Words and Music by
SAM FARRAR, ADAM LEVINE,
JESSE CARMICHAEL, MICHAEL MADDEN
and JAMES VALENTINE

C
B
And I wrote two hun - dred let - ters I will nev - er send.
the way it feels to be com - plete-ly in - ter - twined;
sim.
C
B
Some - times these cuts are so much deep-er then they seem.
not that I did-n't care, it's that I did - n't know.
C
B
You'd rath - er cov-er up; I'd rath - er let them bleed. So
It's not what I did-n't feel, it's what I did - n't show. So

C B7

let me be, and I'll set you free, oh, yeah.

let me be, and I'll set you free.

cresc.

𝄋 *Chorus:*

Em7 Am D7 G

I am in mis - er - y. There

f

Em7 Am D7 G

ain't no - bod - y who can com - fort me, oh, yeah.

Em7
Am
D7
G
3
Why won't you an - swer me? The
To Coda
si - lence is slow - ly kill - ing me, oh, yeah.
Girl, you real - ly got me bad, you real - ly got me bad.
1.
I'm gon - na get you back, gon - na get you back, yeah.

2.

Bridge:

D7 G Bm

now wan-na get you back, yeah.__ You say your faith_ is shak - en,__

Am F♯dim7

and you may be__ mis - tak - en, you keep_ me wide_ a - wake_ and

G Bm

wait - ing for the sun.______ I'm des - p'rate and__ con - fused,_

Am C Am/C Am

so far__ a - way_ from you,_ and I'm get - ting near._ I don't_ care where_

B
B+
B
Breakdown:
N.C.
I have to run.
Why do you
mf
do what-cha do to me, yeah?
Why won't you
Em7
Am
an-swer me, an-swer me, yeah?
Why do you
D7
G
3
Em7
Am
do what-cha do to me, yeah?
Why won't you

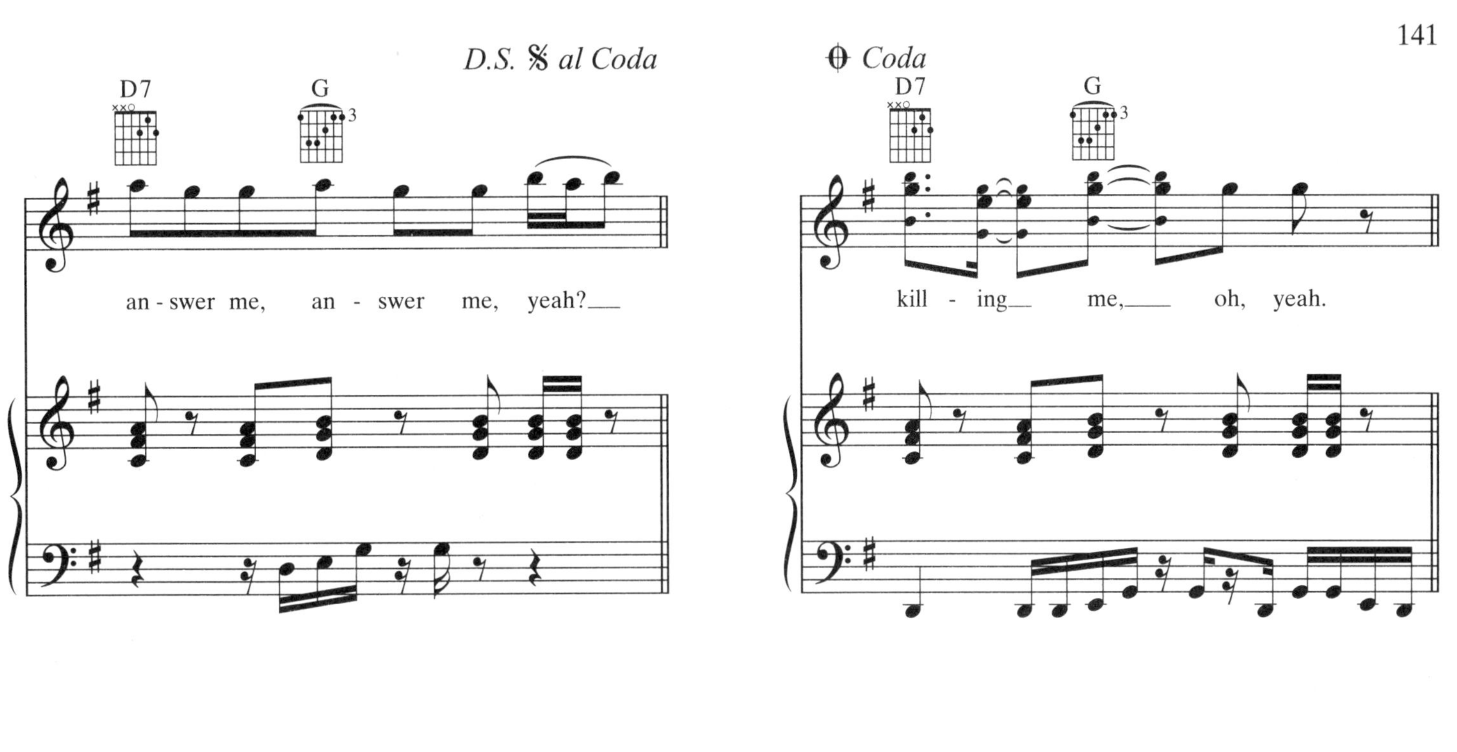
D.S. 𝄋 al Coda
D7
G
3
an - swer me, an - swer me, yeah?
𝄌 Coda
D7
G
3
kill - ing me, oh, yeah.

Outro:
Em7
Am
D7
G
3
Girl, you real - ly got me bad,
you real - ly got me bad.

Repeat and fade
Em7
Am
D7
G
3
I'm gon - na get you back,
now wan - na get you back,
yeah.

NOT LIKE THE MOVIES

Words and Music by
KATY PERRY and GREG WELLS

*2nd time, piano 8vb.

Cm
E♭
A♭5
Fm7
Cm
E♭
know. I don't know,
match, got-ta find my bet-ter half, so we make per-fect shapes.
cresc.
D♭2
E♭sus
Fm7
I did-n't feel the fair-y-tale feel-ing, no.
If stars don't a-lign, if it does-n't stop time, if you can't see the sign,
(loco)
Cm
D♭2
E♭sus
Am I a stu-pid girl for e-ven
wait for it. One hun-dred per-cent, worth ev-'ry pen-ny spent,

Fm7
Cm
E♭
dream - ing that I could?
he'll be the one that fin - ish - es your sen - tenc - es.
Chorus:
A♭5
D♭2
G♭6/9
A♭5
D♭2
If it's not like the mov - ies, that's how it should
G♭6/9
A♭5
D♭2
Fm
Cm
be, yeah. When he's the one, I'll come un - done, and my world will stop

1.
B♭m(9)
A♭/C
D♭maj7
spin - ning.
And that's just the be - gin - ing,
A♭5
Fm7
Cm
E♭
yeah.
2.
gin - ing.
Bridge:
Fm
A♭/E♭
Oh, oh, yeah. 'Cause I know you're out there. And you're,
mf

B♭9/D
B♭m
Fm
3
you're look - ing for me, oh. It's a cra - zy i -
A♭/E♭
B♭7/D
B♭m
A♭/C
D♭
dea that you were made per - fect - ly for me,
Fm
E♭
A♭5
D♭5
you see. Just like the mov -
8va
mp
G♭2
A♭5
D♭5
G♭2
ies, that's how it will be.
(8va)

A♭5
D♭5
Fm
Cm
B♭m(9)
Cin-e-mat-ic and dra-mat-ic, with the per-fect end-ing. Oh, whoa,
A♭
D♭
A♭/G♭
G♭6/9
A♭
D♭
it's not like the mov-ies, but that's how it should
mf
A♭/G♭
G♭6/9
A♭
D♭
Fm
Cm
be, yeah. When he's the one, you'll come un-done, and your world will stop
B♭m(9)
A♭/C
D♭
spin-ning. And it's just the be-gin-ing.
dim.

NEED YOU NOW

Words and Music by
DAVE HAYWOOD, CHARLES KELLEY,
HILLARY SCOTT and JOSH KEAR

*Alternate between open G and A on the 3rd string.

Am
C♯m
Fmaj9
Amaj9
Reach-ing for the phone, 'cause
wish - ing you'd come sweep - ing in
I can't fight it an - y - more.
the way you did be - fore.
Both:
And I won-
der if I ev - er cross your mind.

Fmaj9
Amaj9
For me it hap - pens all the time. It's a
For me it hap - pens all the time. It's a
Chorus:
C
E
Both:
Em
G♯m
quar-ter af - ter one, I'm all a - lone and I need you now.
quar-ter af - ter one, I'm a lit - tle drunk and I need you now.
C
E
I said I would-n't call, but I lost all con - trol and I need
Em
G♯m
you now.
Fmaj9
Amaj9
And I don't know how I can do

1.
with - out.
I just need you now.
Am
C♯m
Male:
2. An -
2.
Am
C♯m
G/B
B/D♯
C
E
just need you now.
(Inst. solo ad lib....
Fmaj9
Amaj9
Gsus
Bsus
Am
C♯m
G/B
B/D♯
C
E
Male:
Whoa, whoa.

Fmaj9
Amaj9
Gsus
Bsus
Both:
...end solo) Guess I'd rath -
Fmaj9
Amaj9
Am
C#m
er hurt than feel noth - ing at all.
mp
Chorus:
Gsus
Bsus
C
E
Female:
It's a quar - ter af - ter one, I'm all a - lone and I need
mf
Em
G#m
C
E
Male:
you now.
And I said I would - n't call, but

Em
G♯m
I'm a lit - tle drunk and I need you now.
Both:
And I don't
Fmaj9
Amaj9
know how I can do with - out.
I just need you now.
C
E
Em
G♯m
I
C
E
just need you now.

Em
G♯m
C
E
Em
G♯m
Female:
Oh, ba - by, I need you now.
C
E
Em
G♯m
C
E
mp

NOTHIN' ON YOU

Words and Music by
PETER HERNANDEZ, PHILIP LAWRENCE,
ARI LEVINE and BOBBY SIMMONS

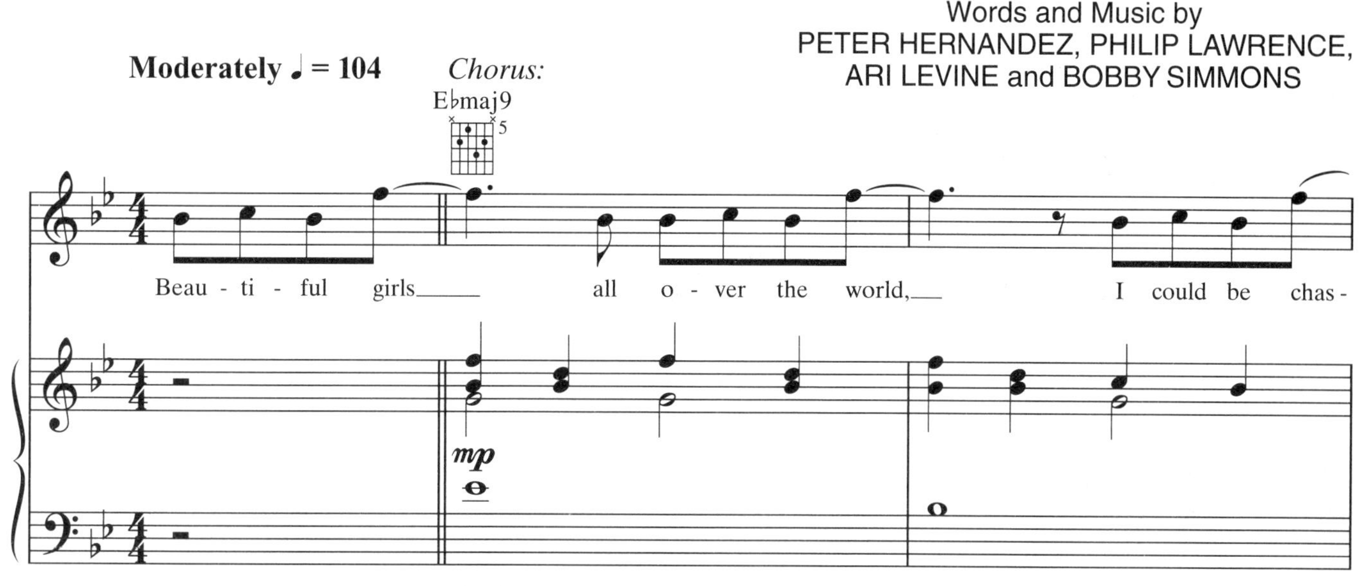

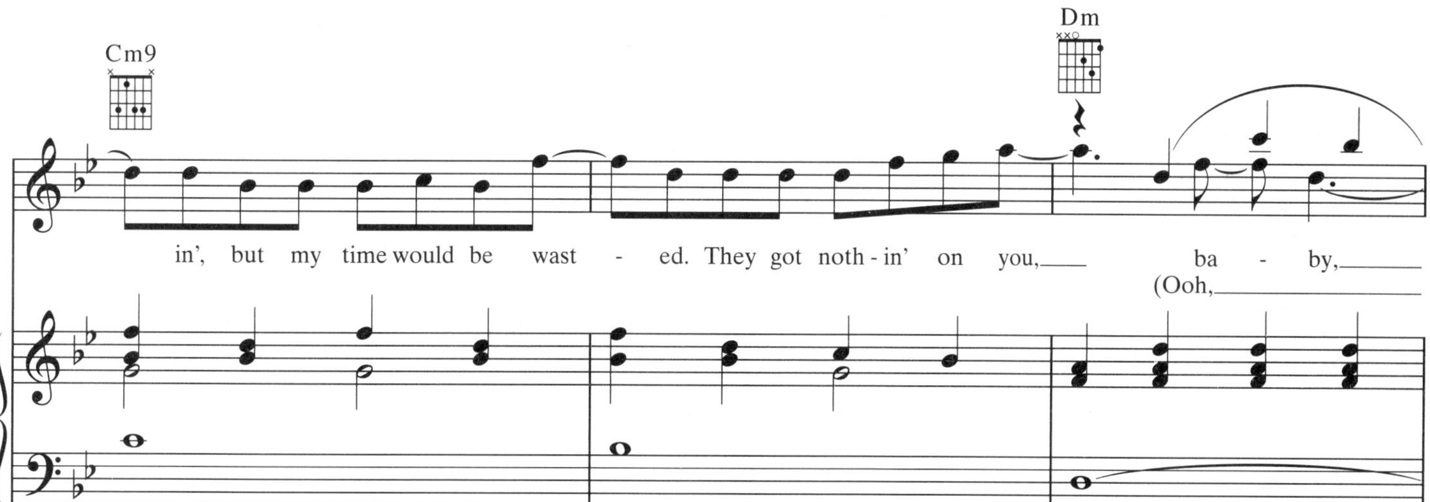

E♭maj9
Cm9
and I might say "Hey," but you should-n't wor - ry a - bout what they say,
Dm
'cause they got noth - in' on you, ba - by, noth - in' on you,
(Ooh,
F
ba - by.
ooh.)
Verse Rap:
E♭maj9
1. I know you feel where I'm coming from, regardless of the things in my past that I've done. Most of it
2. See additional lyrics
mf

Cm9
really was for the hell of the fun. On a carousel,
so around I spun, with no
Dm
direction, just tryin' to get some. Tryin' to chase
skirts, living in the summer sun, and so I
F
lost more than I had ever won,
and honestly, I ended up with none.
1. It's so much
2. I've been to
Pre-chorus:
E♭maj9
non - sense, it's on my con - science. I'm think-ing, may-be I should get it out. And I don't wan-na sound re-
Lon - don, I've been to Par - is, e - ven way out there in To-ky-o. Back home down in

Cm9
dun - dant, but I was won - d'rin' if there was some - thing that you wan - na know. But nev - er mind
Geor - gia, to New Or - leans, but you al - ways steal the show. And just like
Dm
that, we should let it go, 'cause we don't wan - na be a T V ep - i - sode. And all the bad
that, girl, you got me froze, like a Nin - ten - do Six - ty - four. If you nev - er
F
N.C.
thoughts, just let 'em go, go, go.
knew, well, now you know, know, know.
Beau - ti - ful girls
Chorus:
E♭maj9
Cm9
all o - ver the world, I could be chas - in', but my time would be wast -

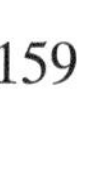

Dm

ed. They got noth - in' on you, ba - by, noth - in' on you,

(Ooh,

F

Ebmaj9

ba - by. They might say "Hi," and I might say "Hey,"

ooh.)

Cm9

but you should-n't wor - ry a - bout what they say, 'cause they got noth - in' on you,

Dm

To Coda 𝄌

F

ba - by, noth - in' on you, ba - by,

(Ooh, ooh.

Bridge:
1.
2.
N.C.
E♭maj9
yeah.
yeah.
)
)
(Ah,
Everywhere I go,
Cm9
ah,
ah,
I'm always hearin' your name.
And no matter where I'm at,
girl, you make me wanna sing.
Dm
Whether a bus or a plane,
or a car, or a train,
ah.
F
N.C.
D.S. 𝄋 al Coda
)
Beau - ti - ful girls
no other girl's on my brain,
and you the one to blame.

Verse 2 Rap:
Hands down, there will never be another one.
I've been around, and I've never seen another one.
Because your style, I ain't really got nothin' on.
And you wild when you ain't got nothin' on.
Baby, you the whole package, plus you pay your taxes,
And you keep it real, while them others stay plastic.
You're my Wonder Woman, call me Mr. Fantastic.
Stop! Now think about it.
(To Pre-chorus:)

THE ONLY EXCEPTION

Words and Music by
HAYLEY WILLIAMS and JOSH FARRO

Verse 1 (sing 1st time only):
B
F♯m6
1. When I was youn - ger, I saw my dad - dy cry and curse at the wind.
Verse 2 (sing 2nd time only):
(2.) may - be I know some - where deep in my soul that love nev - er lasts.
Emaj7
B
He broke his own heart, and I watched as he tried to re -
And we've got to find oth - er ways to make it a - lone,
F♯m6
Emaj7
B
as - sem - ble it. And my ma - ma swore that she
or keep a straight face. And I've al - ways lived like

F♯m6
would nev - er___ let her - self for - get.__
this, keep - ing a com - f'ta - ble
Emaj7
B
And that was the day___ that I
dis - tance. And up un - til now I had sworn__
F♯m6
prom - ised I'd nev - er sing of love if it does not ex -
__ to my - self__ that I'm con - tent___ with lone - li - ness,_

1.
To Next Strain
2.
Emaj7
Emaj7
ist. But, dar - lin', because none of it was ev - er worth the risk. Well,
Chorus:
B
(sing harmony 2nd time)
you are the on - ly ex - cep - tion. Well,
F♯m6
Emaj7
you are the on - ly ex - cep - tion. Well,
B
you are the on - ly ex - cep - tion. Well,

1.
F♯m6
Emaj7
you are the on - ly ex - cep - tion.
2.
B
Emaj7
2. Well, on - ly ex - cep - tion.
C♯m9
B
F♯
C♯m9
B
F♯
I've got a

Bridge:
C♯m9
tight grip on re - al - i - ty, but I can't let
B
go of what's in front of me here.
F♯
I know you're
C♯m9
leav - ing in the morn - ing when you wake up.
Leave me
B
with some kind of proof it's not a
F♯
dream. Oh.

Emaj9
Chorus:
B
(sing harmony 2nd time)
You are the on - ly ex - cep - tion.
F♯m6
Emaj7
You are the on - ly ex - cep - tion.
B
You are the on - ly ex - cep - tion. Well,

1.
F♯m6
Emaj7
you are the on - ly ex - cep - tion.
2.
F♯m6
Emaj7
A
you are the on - ly ex - cep - tion. And I'm on my
Emaj7
B
way to be - liev - ing.
Oh, and
A
Emaj7
B
I'm on my way to be - liev - ing.
mp

PERFECT DAY

Words and Music by
LOU REED

G
Em7
F♯
then lat - er, when it gets dark, we go home.
Bm
E
A
D
Just a per-fect day, feed an - i - mals in the zoo,
G
Em7
F♯
F♯7
then lat - er a mov-ie, too, and then home. Oh,
mf
Chorus:
B
E
D♯m
E
B/D♯
C♯m7
it's such a per-fect day. I'm glad I spent it with you.

B
F♯
G♯m
F♯
E
F♯
Oh, such a per-fect day. You just keep me hang - ing on.__ You just
G♯m
F♯
E
keep me hang - ing on.
Verse 2:
Bm
E
A
D
2. Just a per-fect day, prob-lems left all__ a-lone,
mp
G
Em7
F♯
F♯7
week-end-ers on our own, it's such fun.

Bm
E
A
D
Just a per-fect day, you make me for-get my-self.
G
Em7
F♯
I thought I was some-one else, some-one good. Oh,
cresc.
Chorus:
B
E
D♯m
E
B/D♯
C♯m7
it's such a love-ly day. I'm glad I spent it with you.
mf
B
F♯
G♯m
F♯
E
F♯
Oh, such a per-fect day. You just keep me hang-ing on. You just

G♯m
F♯
E
G♯m
F♯
E
F♯
keep me hang - ing on.
mp cresc. poco a poco
G♯m
F♯
E
F♯
G♯m
F♯
Emaj7
f
F♯/A♯
A6
E
B/D♯
C♯m7
You're gon - na reap just what you sow.
mp
B
F♯/A♯
A
E
B/D♯
C♯m7
You're gon - na reap___ just what you sow.___
(Bkgrd.) Reap, reap, reap, sow.___

B
F♯/A♯
A
E
B/D♯
C♯m7
You're gon - na reap just what you sow.
Reap, reap, reap, sow.
cresc. poco a poco
B
F♯/A♯
A
E
B/D♯
C♯m7
You're gon - na reap just what you sow.
Reap, reap, reap just what you sow, oh.
mf
cresc.
B
F♯/A♯
A
E
B/D♯
C♯m7
B
You're gon - na reap just what you sow.
Reap, reap, reap just what you sow.
f
molto rit. e dim.
mp

RHYTHM OF LOVE

Words and Music by
TIM LOPEZ

A♭
E♭7
Fm
E♭
warm sun and wind in my ear. We'll watch the world from a-bove
D♭
E♭
A♭
A♭7
as it turns to the rhy-thm of love." We may
Chorus:
D♭
A♭
on-ly have to-night, but 'til the
D♭
A♭
C7
morn-ing sun, you're mine, all

Fm
E♭
D♭
E♭
E♭7
mine. Play the mu - sic low and sway to the rhy-thm of
A♭
E♭7
A♭
E♭7
love.
Verse 2:
A♭
E♭7
A♭
E♭7
2. Well, my heart beats like a drum, a gui - tar string to the strum, a
Fm
E♭
D♭
E♭
beau - ti - ful song to be sung. She's got

A♭
E♭7
A♭
E♭7
blue eyes deep like the sea that roll back when she's laugh-ing at me. She
Fm
E♭
D♭
E♭
ris - es up like the tide the mo - ment her lips meet
Chorus:
A♭
A♭7
D♭
mine. We may on - ly have to - night,
A♭
D♭
but 'til the morn - ing sun you're mine,

A♭
C7/G
Fm
E♭
all mine. Play the mu - sic low
D♭
E♭
E♭7
To Coda
A♭
E♭7
and sway to the rhy-thm of love.
Bridge:
A♭
E♭7
C7
D♭
When the moon is
A♭
E♭/G
C7
D♭
low, we can dance in

A♭
E♭/G
D♭
slow mo - tion and all your
E♭
D♭
tears will sub - side. All your
Verse 3:
E♭
A♭
E♭7
tears will dry. 3. Bop ba.
Bop ba, bop ba.
A♭
E♭7
Fm
E♭
Bop ba. Da da da dum da da
Bop ba, bop ba.

D♭
E♭
A♭
E♭7
dum.
Bop ba.
Bop ba, bop ba.
A♭
E♭7
Fm
E♭
Bop ba.
Bop ba, bop ba.
Da da da dum da da
D♭
E♭
A♭
E♭7
dum.
And long af - ter I've gone,
A♭
E♭7
Fm
E♭
you'll still be hum-ming a - long. And I will keep you in my

D.S. 𝄋 al Coda
N.C.
D♭
E♭
A♭
mind, the way you make love so fine. We may
𝄌 Coda
A♭
E♭7
Fm
E♭
love. Oh, play the mu - sic low
D♭
E♭
E♭7
A♭
E♭7
and sway to the rhy-thm of love.
A♭
E♭7
A♭
E♭7
A♭
Yeah, sway to the rhy-thm of love.

ROCKETEER

Words and Music by
JONATHAN YIP, JEREMY REEVES, RAY ROMULUS,
PHILIP LAWRENCE, PETER HERNANDEZ, JAMES ROH, JAE CHOUNG,
KEVIN NISHIMURA and VERMAN COQUIA

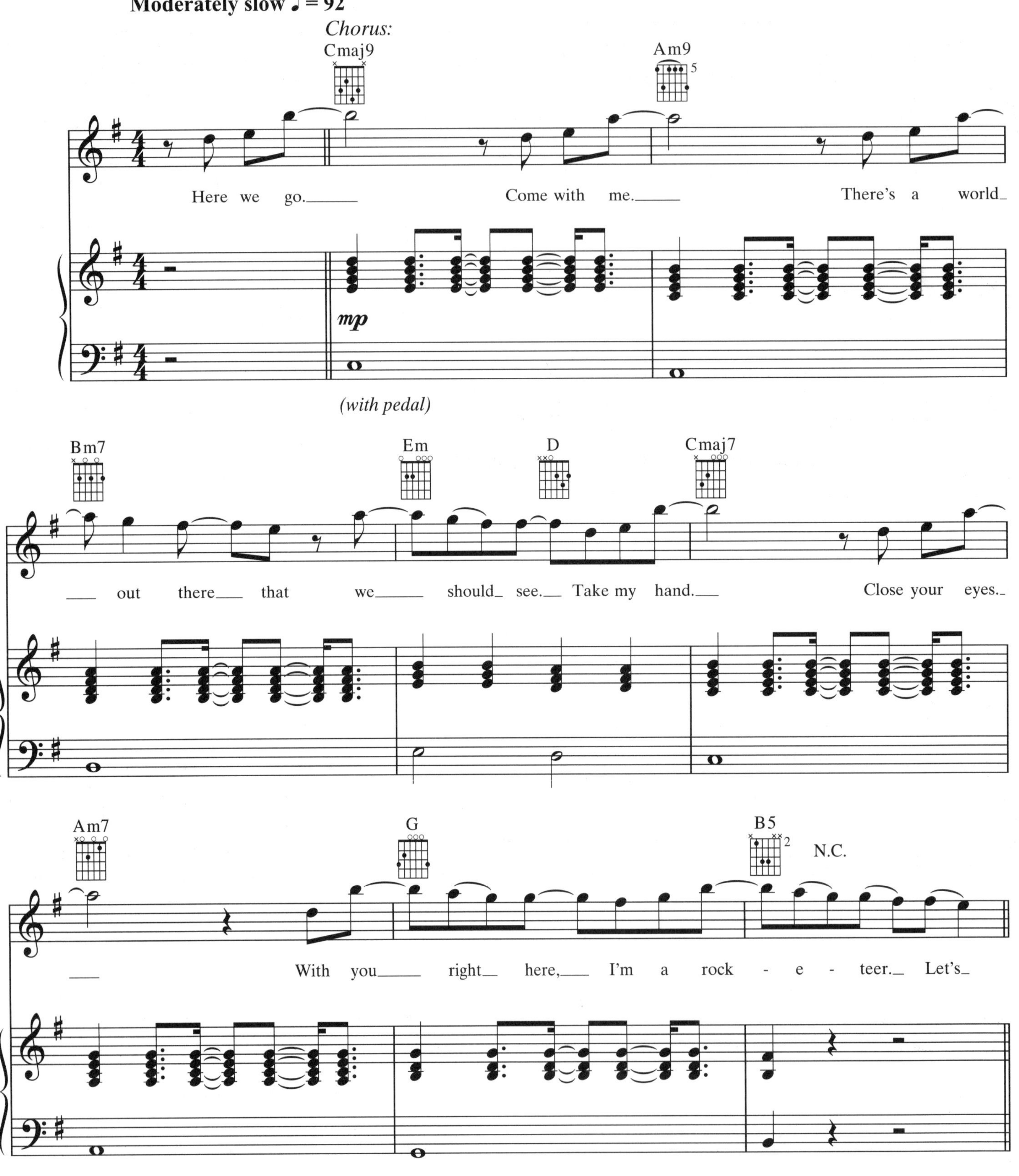

Cmaj9
Am9
fly.
Fly,
fly,
fly,
fly.
mf
Bm7
Em
D
Up, up, here we go, go.
Up, up, here we go, go.
Let's
Cmaj7
Am7
fly.
Fly,
fly,
fly,
fly.
G
To Coda
B7
Up, up, here we go, go. Where we stop, no - bod - y knows, knows.
1. Where we
2. Ba - by,

Verse:
Cmaj9
Am9
go, we don't need roads,___ and where we stop, no - bod - y knows. To the
2. See additional lyrics
Bm7
Em
D
stars, if you real - ly want it. Got, got a jet - pack with your name on it. A - bove the
Cmaj7
Am7
clouds in the at - mo - sphere, just say the words and we out - ta here. Hold my
G
B7
hand if you're feel - ing scared. We're fly - ing up, up, out - ta here. Here we go.___

Chorus:
Cmaj9
Am9
Bm7
Come with me.
There's a world out there that we
Em
D
Cmaj7
Am7
should see. Take my hand.
Close your eyes.
With you
G
N.C.
1.
2.
B7
right here, I'm a rock - e - teer. Let's
e - teer. Let's
Bridge:
Cmaj9
Am9
Bm7
fly. Now, I never been in space before. But I ain't never seen a face like yours. You make me feel like I can touch the planets.

Em
D
Cmaj7
Am7
You want the moon, girl, watch me grab it.
See, I never seen a star this close.
You got me stuck by the way you glow.
G
N.C.
Chorus:
Cmaj9
I'm like, oh, oh, oh, oh.
I'm like, oh, oh, oh, oh.
Here we go.
Come with me.
Am9
Bm7
There's a world out there that we
Em
D
Cmaj7
should see. Take my hand.
Close your eyes.

Verse 2:
Baby, we can stay fly like a G6,
Shop the streets of Tokyo, get your fly kicks.
Girl, you're always on my mind.
Got my head up in the sky,
And I'm never looking down, feeling priceless, yeah.
Where we at, only few have known.
Go on the next level, Super Mario.
I hope this works out cardio.
'Til then, let's fly.
Geronimo.
(To Chorus:)

TEMPORARY HOME

Words and Music by
CARRIE UNDERWOOD, LUKE LAIRD
and ZAC MALOY

Fmaj9
an - oth - er school, an - oth - er house that - 'll nev - er be home.
'cause a half - way house will nev - er be a home.
Am
Em7/G
When peo - ple ask him how he likes this place,
At night she whis - pers to her ba - by girl,
Fmaj9
Am
he looks up and says with a smile
Some - day we'll find our place
Em7/G
Fmaj9
up - on his face,
here in this world.
This is my tem - po - rar - y home,
This is our tem - po - rar - y home,

Chorus:
C
Gsus/B
it's not where I be - long.
it's not where we be - long.
Win - dows and rooms
Win - dows and rooms
Am
Em7/G
Fmaj9
that I'm pass - ing through.
that we're pass - ing through.
This is just a stop
This is just a stop
C
G/B
on the way to where I'm go - ing.
on the way to where we're go - ing.
I'm not a - fraid
I'm not a - fraid
Am
Em7/G
Fmaj9
be - cause I know
be - cause I know
this is my
this is our

1.
Gsus
C(9)
Fmaj9
tem-po-rar - y home.
Mm.
2.
G
C
tem - po - rar - y home.
G/B
Am
Em7/G
Fmaj9
decresc.
Verse 3:
C5
Fmaj9
3. Old man, hos - pi - tal bed, the room is filled with peo-ple he loves.
mp

Am
Em7/G
And he whis - pers, "Don't cry for me I'll see you all some day."
Fmaj9
Am7
He looks up and says, "I
G
Fmaj9
can see God's face."
This is my tem - po - rar - y home,
Chorus:
C5
C/B
Am
it's not where I be - long.
Win - dows and rooms
that I'm pass - ing through,

Fmaj9
C
G/B
this was just a stop on the way to where I'm go - ing. I'm not a - fraid
mf
Am
Em7/G
Fmaj9
Gsus
be - cause I know this was my tem - po - rar -
C(9)
C
Fmaj9
y home. Mm.
C(9)
C
Fmaj9
This is our tem - po - rar - y home.

WAKE UP EVERYBODY

Words and Music by
GENE McFADDEN, JOHN WHITEHEAD
and VICTOR CARSTARPHEN

*Recorded in E♭ minor.

Dm7
Gm7
Dm7
Gm7
world has changed_ so ver - y much_ from what it used_ to be.____
they don't have____ so ver - y long__ be - fore their Judg - ment_ Day, so
Dm7
Gm7
Gm7/C
There is so____ much ha - tred, war, and pov - er - ty.____
won't you make_ them hap - py be - fore they pass a - way.____
1.
To Next Strain
Oh,____ oh,__ yeah,____ yeah.__
2.
Verses 2 & 4:
Dm7
Gm7
Oh, yeah.____
2. Wake up, all the teach - ers, time to
4. Wake up, all the build - ers, time to

Dm7
Gm7
Dm7
Gm7
teach a new way.
build a new land.
May - be then they'll lis - ten to
I know we can do it if we
Gm7/C
Dm7
Gm7
what you have to say.
all lend a hand.
'Cause they're the ones who's com - in' up, and the
The on - ly thing we have to do is
Dm7
Gm7
Dm7
Gm7
world is in their hands.
put it in our minds.
When you teach the chil - dren, teach them the
Sure - ly, things will work out, 'cause they
Gm7/C
ver - y best you can.
do ev - 'ry time.
Oh, yeah.
Yeah.

Chorus:
B♭maj7
C
Am7
D7
Gm7
C
The world won't get no bet - ter
if we just let it be.
F
F7
B♭maj7
C
Am7
D7
The world won't get no bet - ter.
You got-ta
Gm7
Gm7/C
1.
F
Gm7/F
F
Gm7/F
change it, yeah, just you and me.
2.
F
Gm7/F
F
Gm7/F

F
Gm7/F
F
Gm7/F
Dm7
Gm7
Dm7
Gm7
Dm7
Gm7
Dm7
Gm7
(Rap - See additional lyrics)
Dm7
Gm7
Dm7
Gm7
Dm7
Gm7
Dm7
Gm7
Dm7
Gm7
Dm7
Gm7
Dm7
Gm7
Dm7
Gm7
Dm7
Gm7
Dm7
Gm7
Dm7
Gm7

Dm7
Gm7
Ah, wake up, ev - 'ry - bod - y, no more sleep - in' in bed. Oh,
wake up, ev - 'ry - bod - y.
Be-cause I need a lit - tle
(Bkgrd. vcl.)
Wake up, ev - 'ry - bod - y.
Ba do ba do, ba do ba do.
help. I can't do it a - lone. Oh, I need a lit - tle
Wake up, ev - 'ry - bod - y, no more sleep - in' in bed.

Dm7
Gm7
Dm7
Gm7
help, y'all. Come on, come on, come on, come on. I need a lit - tle
Wake up, ev - 'ry - bod - y. Ba do ba do, ba do ba do.
Dm7
Gm7
Dm7
Gm7
help, y'all. Can't do it a - lone. Oh, I need a lit - tle
Oh.
Dm7
Gm7
Dm7
Gm7
help, y'all, can't do it a - lone.
Wake up, ev - 'ry - bod - y. Ba do ba do, ba do ba do.

Rap:
It's the God hour,
The morning, I wake up.
Just for the breath of life, I thank my Maker.
My mom say I come from hustlers and shakers.
My mom built it on skyscrapers and acres.
He said, take us back to where we belong.
I try to write a song as sweet as the Psalms,
Though I'm the type to bear arms
And wear my heart on my sleeve.
Even when I fail, in God I believe.
Read the days that weave through the maze
And the seasons so amazing.
Feed them and raise them,
Seasons are aging.
Earthquakes, wars, and rumors.
I want us to get by, but
We more than consumers,
We more than shooters, more than looters.
Created in this image so God live through us.
And even in this generation, living through computers,
Only love, love, love can reboot us.

SMILE

Words and Music by
MATTHEW SHAFER, BLAIR DALY,
J.T. HARDING and JEREMY BOSE

Verses 1 (cont.) & 2:
E
F♯m9
Amaj9
(1.) Com-plete-ly un - a - ware, noth-ing can com-pare to where_ you send_
2. E - ven when you're gone, some-how you come a - long just like__ a flow-
B
A
F♯m7(4)
A
__ me, lets__ me know_ that it's__ o - kay.____ yeah, it's__ o - kay,__ in the
er pok - ing through_ the side - walk____ crack, and just__ like that,_____ you
mf
B
A
F♯m7(4)
N.C.
mo-ments when_ my good_ times start to fade.____
steal a - way__ the rain,__ and just like that...____
You make_ me smile_
Chorus:
E
B
A
F♯m7
__ like the sun, fall__ out of bed, sing___ like a bird, diz - zy in my head, spin_
f

E
B
A
F♯m7
like a rec-ord, cra - zy on a Sun - day night.
You make me dance
E
B
C♯m7
A
like a fool, for - get how to breathe, shine like gold, buzz like a bee.
E
B
1.
A
F♯m7
N.C.
Just the thought of you can drive me wild.
Oh, you make me
E
F♯m9
Amaj9
smile.
mp

2.
Bridge:
A
F♯m7
C♯m
C♯m7/B
wild.
Oh, you make me
smile.
Don't know how I live with-out you,
F♯9/A♯
C♯m
C♯m7/B
'cause ev-'ry time that I get a-round you
I see the best of me in-side your eyes.
F♯9/A♯
Amaj9
You make me
smile.
B
E
F♯m9
You make me dance like a fool, for-get how to breathe, shine
mp

Amaj9
E
F♯m9
like gold, buzz like a bee. Just the thought of you can drive me wild.
Chorus:
Amaj9
E
B
You make me smile like the sun, fall out of bed, sing
f
A
F♯m7
E
B
like a bird, diz - zy in my head, spin like a rec-ord, cra - zy on a Sun - day night.
A
F♯m7
E
B
You make me dance like a fool, for - get how to breathe, shine

C♯m7
4
A
E
B
like gold, buzz like a bee. Just the thought of you can drive me
A
F♯m7
E
F♯m9
wild. Oh, you make me smile.
Oh, you make me
mf
Amaj9
E
F♯m9
Oh, you make me smile.
smile. Oh, you make me
Amaj9
N.C.
Oh, you make me smile.
smile.

BORN THIS WAY

Words and Music by
FERNANDO GARIBAY, STEFANI GERMANOTTA,
JEPPE LAURSEN and PAUL BLAIR

Moderate dance beat ♩ = 120

C♯m

mp

(Spoken:) It doesn't matter if you love him, *or capital H.I.M.*

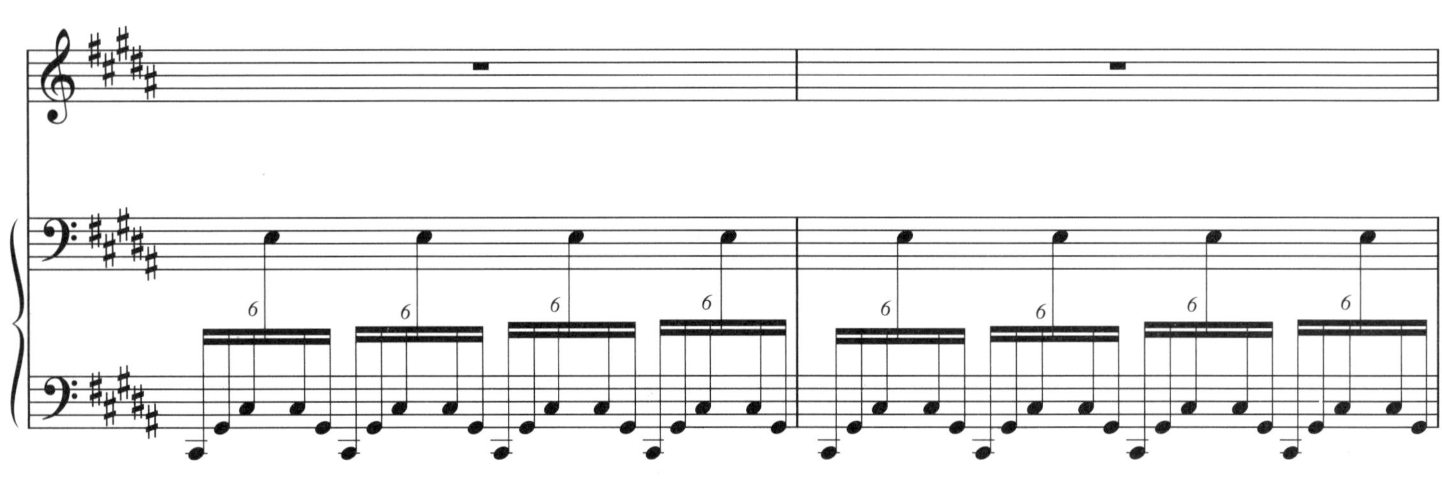

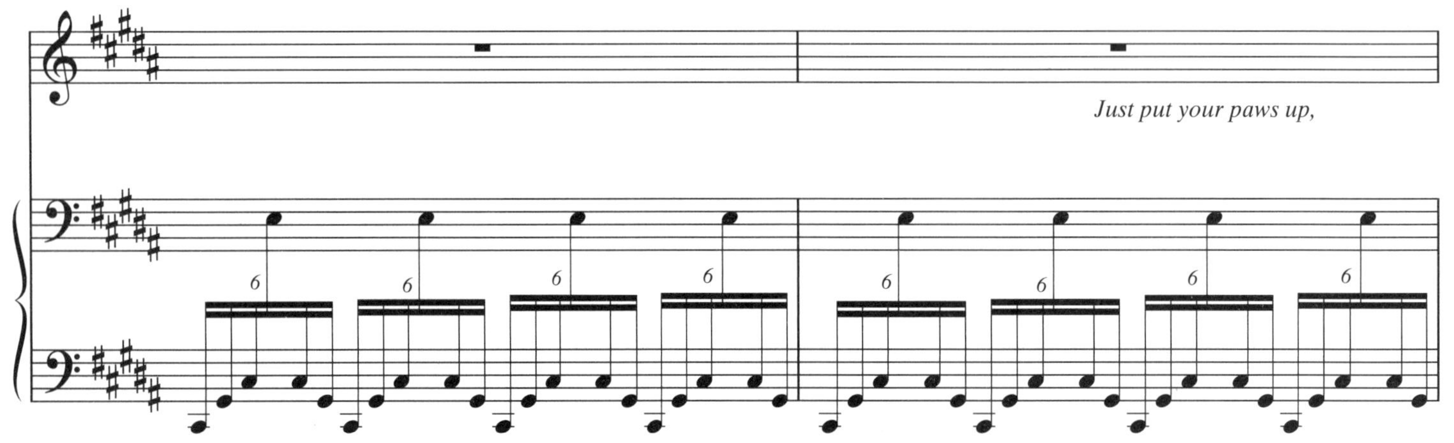

B5
'cause you were born this way, baby.
6
cresc.
F♯5
E5
B5
mf
Verse:
F♯5
F♯
E
1. My ma-ma told me when I was young,
2. Give your-self pru-dence, and love your friends.
B
F♯
we're all born su-per-stars.
Sub-way kid, re-joice your truth.
She rolled my hair and put my
In the re-li-gion of the

E
B
lip - stick_ on___ in the glass of her bou - doir.
in - se - cure,___ I must be my - self, re - spect my youth.
F♯5
E5
"There's noth - ing wrong with lov - in' who you are,"___ she said,
A dif - f'rent lov - er___ is not a sin.___ Be - lieve
B5
"'cause He made you per - fect, babe.
cap - i - tal H. I.___ M. (Hey.___)
F♯5
E5
So, hold your head up, girl, and you'll go___ far.___
I love my life, I love this rec - ord___ and,___ mi

𝄋 *Chorus:*

B5 N.C. F♯

Lis-ten to me when I say..."
a-mo-re vo-le fe yah. *(Whispered:) Same DNA.* } I'm beau-ti-ful in my way, 'cause God makes

E B F♯

no mis-takes. I'm on the right track, ba-by, I was born this way. Don't hide your-

E B

self in re-gret. Just love your-self and you're set. I'm on the right track, ba-by, I was

F♯ E

born this way. Born this way.
Ooh, there ain't no oth-er way, ba-by, I was born this way.

B
F♯
Ba - by, I was born this way.
(Born this way.)
Ooh, there ain't no oth - er way,
To Coda
1.
E
B
F♯
ba - by, I was born this way.
Right track, ba - by, I was born this way.
Don't
N.C.
be a drag, just be a queen. Don't be a drag, just be a queen. Don't be a drag, just be a queen. Don't
2.
F♯
C♯m
be, don't be, don't be.
born this way.
mp

Don't
Bridge:
be a drag, just be a queen, wheth - er you're broke or ev - er - green, you're
black, white, beige, Cho - la de - scent, you're Leb - a - nese, you're O - ri - ent. Wheth -
F♯5
er life's dis - a - bil - i - ties left you out - cast, bull - ied, or teased, re -
mf

F♯
joice and love your - self to - day, 'cause, ba - by, you were born this way.
No mat - ter
F♯5
E5
B5
gay, straight, or bi, les - bi - an, trans-gen-dered life, I'm on the right track, ba - by, I was
F♯5
born to sur - vive. No mat - ter black, white, or beige, Cho - la or
E5
B5
N.C.
D.S. 𝄋 al Coda
Or - i - ent made, I'm on the right track, ba - by, I was born to be brave. I'm beau-ti -

𝄌 Coda

F♯ E

born_ this way._ I was born this way, hey._ I was born this way, hey._ I'm on the

B F♯ N.C.

right track, ba - by, I was born this way, hey._ I was born this way, hey._ I was

born this way, hey._ I'm on the right track, ba - by, I was born this way, hey._

Repeat ad lib. and fade

F♯ F♯m F♯ F♯m

(Spoken:) Same DNA, *but born this way.*

mp

YOU HAVEN'T SEEN THE LAST OF ME

Words and Music by
DIANE WARREN

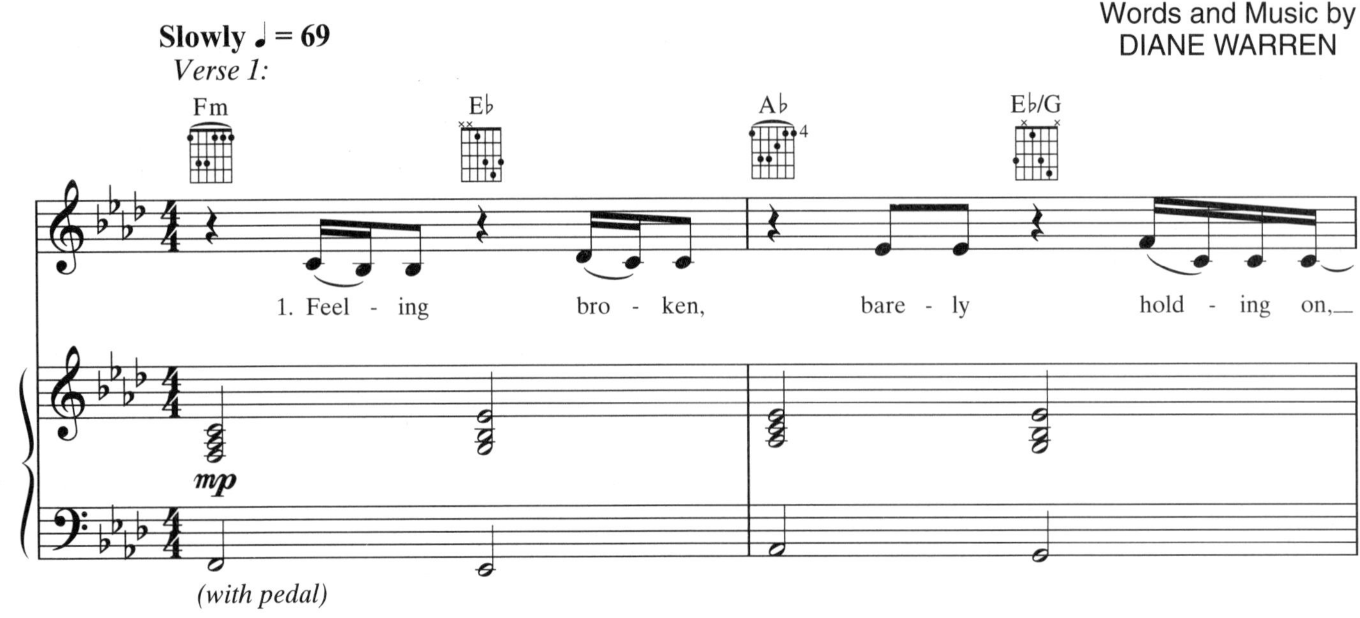

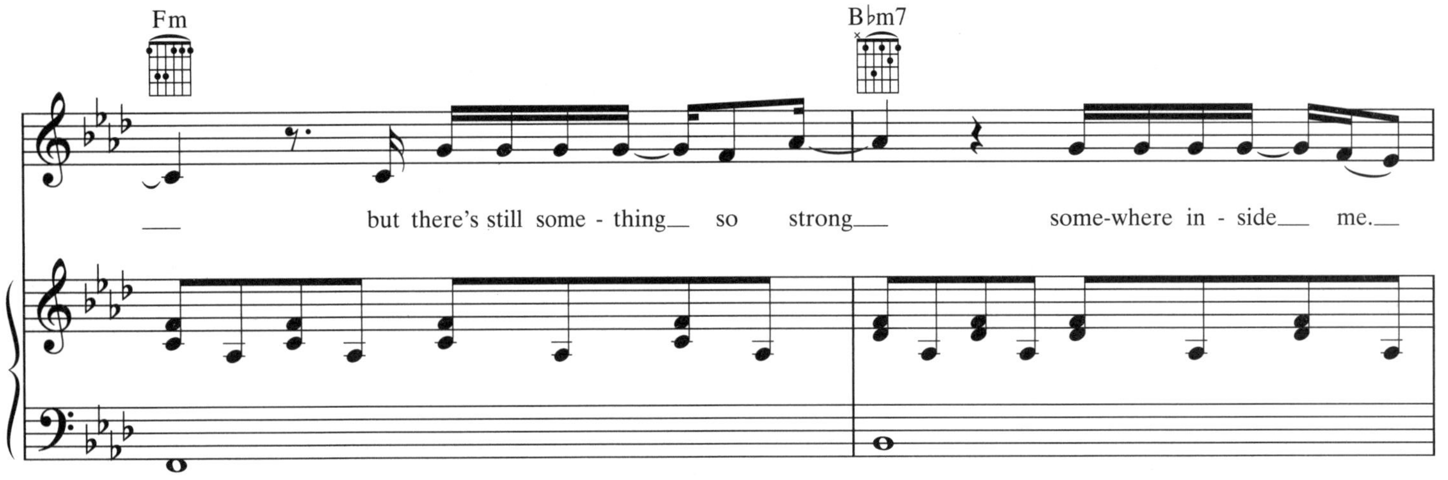

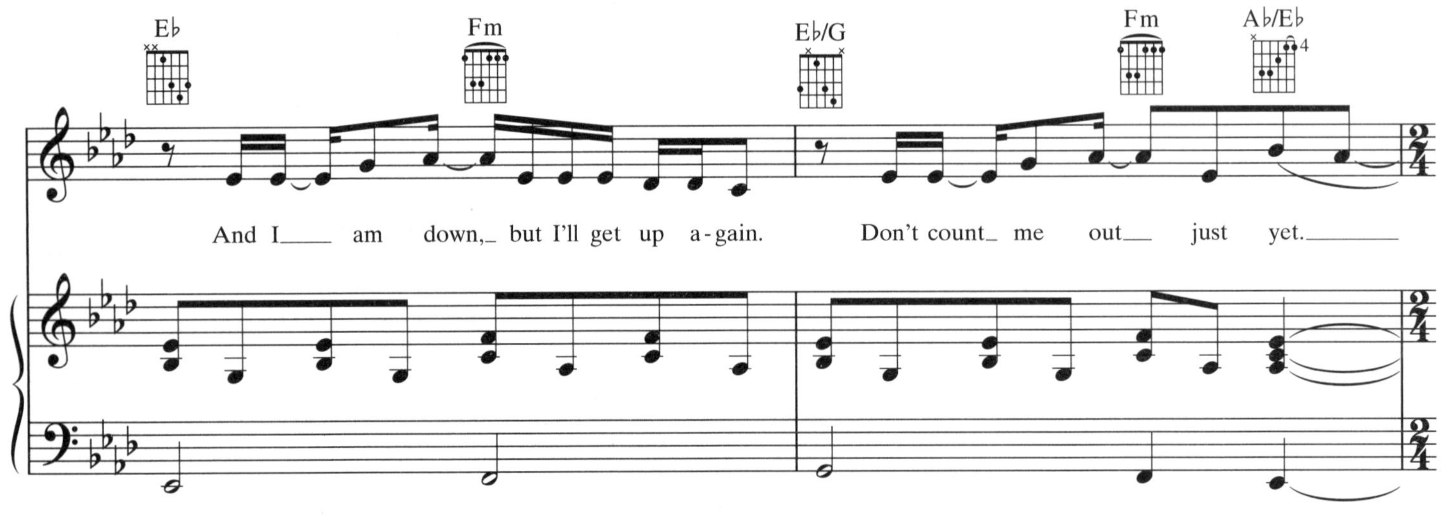

Chorus:

D♭

I've been brought ___ down to my

a tempo

A♭/C B♭m7

knees. And I've been pushed way past ___ the point ___

A♭ D♭

of break - ing, but I can take ___ it. I'll be back, ___ back ___ on my

A♭ B♭m7 E♭

feet. This is far from o - ver. You have - n't seen the last of me. ___

Verse 2:
Db
Fm
Eb
You have-n't seen the last of me.
2. They can say that
mf
Ab
Eb/G
Fm
I won't stay a-round,
but I'm gon-na stand my ground.
Bbm7
Eb
Fm
You're not gon-na stop me.
You don't know me, you don't know who I am.
Eb/G
Fm
Eb
Don't count me out so fast.
I've been

Chorus:

Db Ab/C

brought___ down to my knees. And I've been

Bbm7 Ab

pushed way past_ the point_ of break - ing, but I can take_ it. I'll be

Db Ab/C

back,___ back on_ my feet. This is far from o -

Bbm7 Eb

ver. You have - n't seen the last of me.

Bridge:

Db Ab/C

There will be no fade out. This is not the end._

Fm
Eb/G
Bbm7
Ab/C
I'm down now, but I'll be stand - ing tall a - gain._ Times are hard, but I was built tough.
Ebsus
N.C.
I'm gon - na show you all what I'm made_ of. I've been
rit.
Chorus:
Eb
Bb/D
brought down to my knees. I've been
a tempo
Cm7
Bb/D
pushed way past_ the point_ of break - ing, but I can take_ it. I'll be

E♭ B♭/D

back, back on my feet. This is far from o -

Cm7

ver. I am far from o - ver.

F E♭ B♭/D

You have - n't seen the last of me. No, no, I'm not go - ing no - where.

mp *f*

Cm7 B♭/D E♭ B♭/D

I'm stay - ing right here. Oh, no. You won't see me fade out.

Cm7
B♭/D
E♭
B♭/F
B♭
I'm not tak-ing my bow.
Can't stop me. It's not
Fsus
F
the end.
You have-n't seen the last of
C5
B♭5
me.
Oh, no, you have-n't seen the last
mp
C
of me. You have-n't seen the last of me.
rit.

 Published by Summit Studios Press.
ISBN: 9780999030509

To my loving family & friends, who helped me find them all.
-M.C.

From lands near and far away,

the animals have gone astray.

Tall, furry, slimy, small,

see if you can count them all.

1
MONKEY
in a
suit

Also find...
1 plant
1 flag
1 brown
paper bag

2
LIZARDS
in a boot

Also find...
2 pots
2 pans
2 tomato
sauce cans

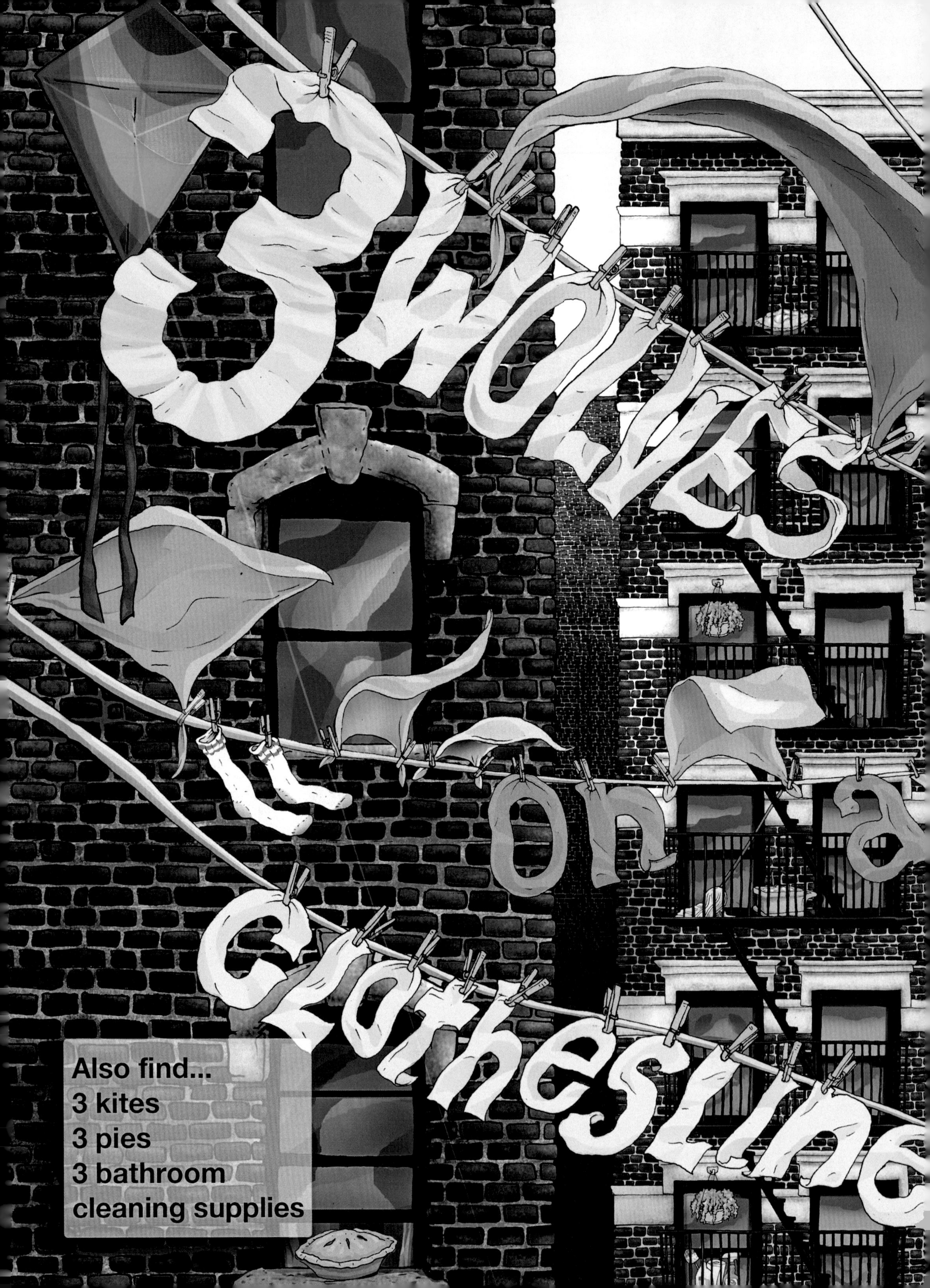
3 Wolves on a Clothesline
Also find...
3 kites
3 pies
3 bathroom
cleaning supplies

4
PANDAS
in a
coal mine
Also find...
4 hammers
4 picks
4 red dynamite
sticks

5
BEAVERS
in a
hamper

Also find...
5 buttons
5 bucks
5 yellow
rubber ducks
NEW
Bio

Also find...
6 acorns
6 forks
6 sparkling
fireworks

ELEPHANTS
in a
camper.
TNT

7 OWLS:
on a
Sled!

Also find...
7 feathers
7 skis
7 pine cones
in trees

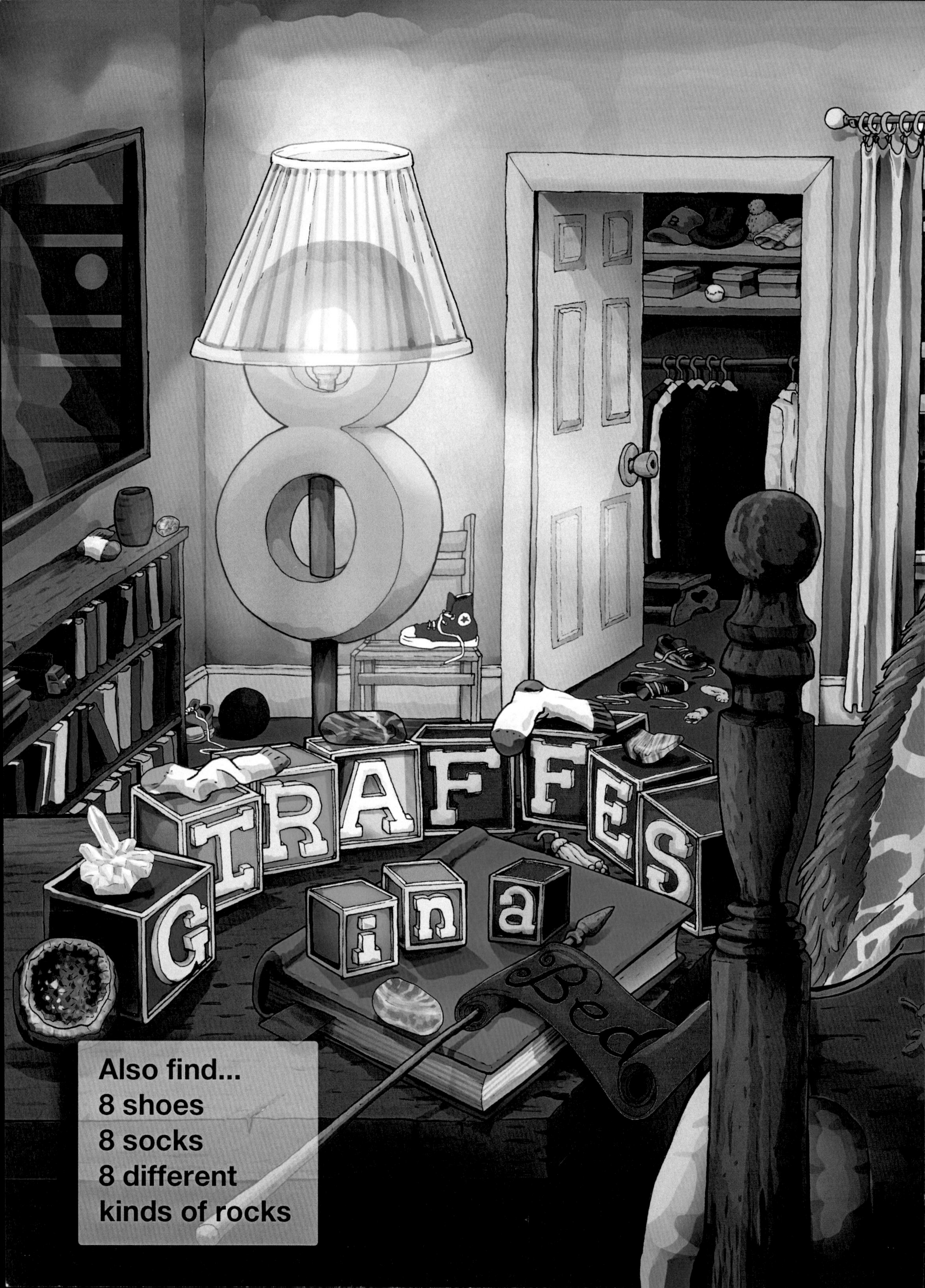
8
GIRAFFES
in a
Bed
Also find...
8 shoes
8 socks
8 different
kinds of rocks

Hope, Charity & Love
WA
OR
ID
NV
CA
AZ
HI

9
FROGS
in a
cookie jar
Baking Soda
Also find...
9 toothpicks
9 spoons
9 colorful
party balloons

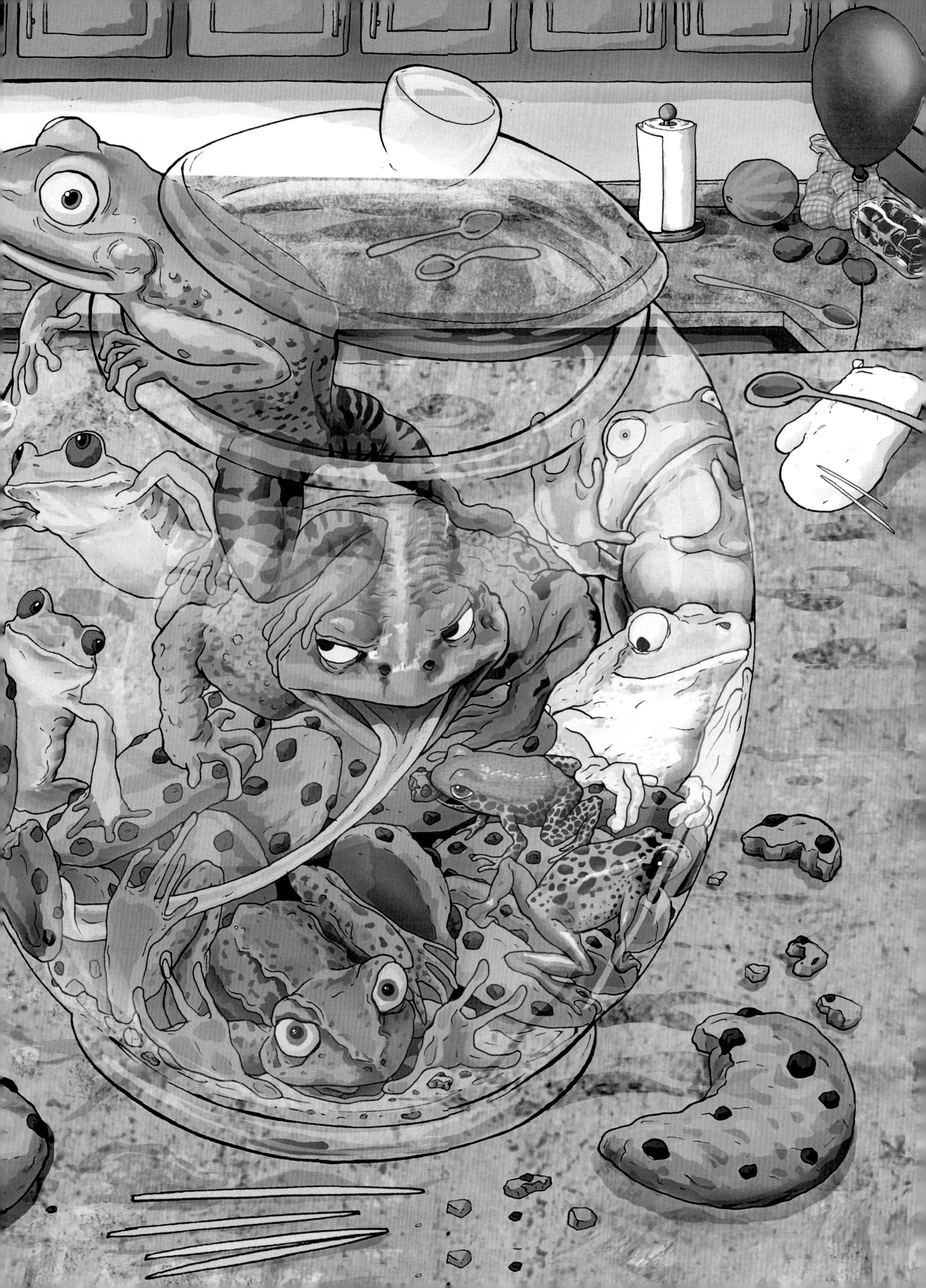

10

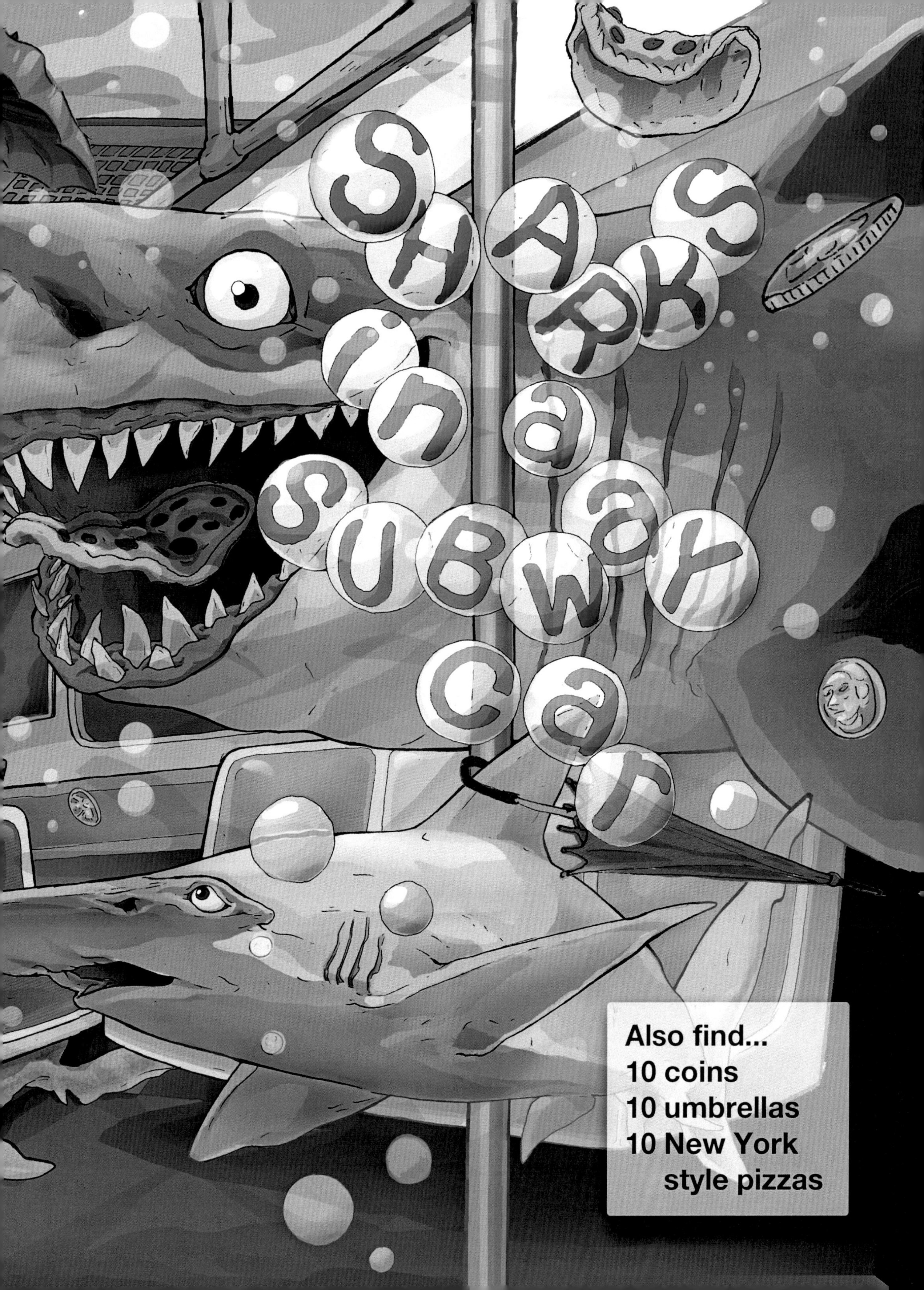
Sharks in a subway car
Also find...
10 coins
10 umbrellas
10 New York
style pizzas

Now you've found them one by one,

and your search is finally done!

Be alert and stay aware,

animals are...

Everywhere

1 Monkey
2 Lizards
3 Wolves
4 Pandas
5 Beavers
6 Elephants
7 Owls
8 Giraffes
9 Frogs
10 Sharks

ABOUT THE ANIMALS

Monkeys

It might be easy to find one monkey in a suit, but it's harder to spot one in the wild. Some monkeys live on the ground, while others live in trees. Most monkeys have tails, and all of them love to eat and play. Old World monkeys live in Africa and Asia and New World monkeys live in South America. Monkeys eat fruit, insects, flowers, leaves, and reptiles. Sorry lizard friends! Half the species of monkeys in the world are threatened with extinction due to habitat loss and hunting. You can help by learning about monkeys and sharing your knowledge with friends and family!

Lizards

Lizards are reptiles. We see reptiles like lizards, snakes, and turtles everywhere, in books, on TV, and in our favorite boots, I mean pet stores! But, that doesn't mean that reptiles can't be endangered. Reptiles around the world are facing the possibility of extinction due to habitat loss and pollution. Some of the most endangered reptiles are the San Francisco Garter Snake, Green Sea Turtles, and the worlds largest lizard the Komodo Dragon which inspired Godzilla! There are many ways we can help protect these endangered species.

Wolves

You won't find wolves hanging around apartment buildings, but you can find their relatives close to home; dogs! One of the worlds most endangered wolves is the Ethiopian Wolf with fewer than 500 left on earth. Located way up in the highlands of Ethiopia, it is the only species to live at such high altitude. The Red Wolf and Mexican Gray Wolf are also endangered, but thanks to the success of conservation efforts many endangered wolves are being saved.

Pandas

Everyone loves pandas and they look especially huggable except when covered in coal mine soot! Pandas come from the mountains of China and eat bamboo. The giant panda is one of the worlds most beloved icons and symbols of peace; in fact, hundreds of years ago warring tribes in China would raise a flag with a picture of a panda on it to stop a battle or call a truce! The giant panda has recently been moved from "endangered" to "vulnerable" which shows that when science, politicians, and local communities come together, we can save our planets endangered species! You can even adopt a panda through the Smithsonian National Zoo!

Beavers

Did you know that a beaver's large front teeth never stop growing and are perfect for chomping through trees, branches, and even laundry baskets? Beavers have bodies that are built for swimming. Their rudder-like tails and webbed feet propel them through the water at 5 miles per hour, and they can stay under for 15 minutes at a time! Beavers also use their tails to slap the water to startle predators. Beavers are very important to reviving streams and their ponds create wetlands. Beavers became endangered in the 1800's due to the fur trade when beaver hats were the height of fashion. Today, beavers are again common throughout the United States!

Elephants

Elephants are the largest land animals in the world and too big to fit into most campers! The largest on record weighed 24,000 pounds and stood 13 feet tall at the shoulder! Elephants are very smart and have lots of personality. They cry, play, have incredible memories, and even laugh. Elephants can live to be over 70 years old, and their skin grows an inch thick. An elephant uses its trunk to lift food and suck up water, then spray it into its mouth to drink. They even use their trunk to breathe like a snorkel in deep water. Elephants are still endangered animals due to poachers who sell their valuable ivory tusks. By educating ourselves we may be able to help.

Owls

Owls do not actually do much sledding,especially during the day! Owls are nocturnal which means they are active at night. They eat insects, small mammals, birds, and fish. Owls can turn their heads as much as 270 degrees around and can fly almost silently. The Barn, Snowy, and Northern Spotted Owl are considered endangered. They suffer due to the destruction of their natural habitat. It isn't too late to help, and the more we learn the more we can be a part of the solution.

Giraffes

The giraffe is the tallest land animal. They spend most of their time on their feet with legs averaging 6 feet tall. In fact, you're unlikely to find giraffes in your bed because they even sleep standing up! Giraffes love to eat leaves. Their long necks help them reach high leafy branches, and they can stretch their toungues out up to a foot and a half to get the really hard to reach ones. Unfortunately, the giraffe has recently been moved from a species of "least concern" to "vulnerable" status. That means that giraffes could face extinction in the wild if nothing is done to protect their habitat and stop poaching.

Frogs

A group of fish is called a school, a group of cattle is called a herd, but a group of frogs is called an army. The army of frogs in this book is easier to find than the most endangered frogs like the Lemur Leaf Frog, The Black-Eyed Leaf Frog and the Harlequin Frog found in parts of Central and South America. These species have suffered from habitat loss due to logging, farming, and water pollution. Frogs are particularly susceptible to the chemicals used in pesticides. You can help your local amphibians by avoiding harsh pesticides in your backyard, and by choosing more organic foods at the grocery store.

Sharks

Did you know sharks never run out of teeth and can grow and lose 20,000 in their lifetime? The average shark lives to be 25 years old, but some can get as old as 100! There are over 400 known species of sharks! The Great White Shark is the biggest of the 10 you'll find in this book. They can be up to 20 feet in length and weigh over 5000 pounds. Although they've never been seen on the subway eating pizza, they're found in all oceans around the world and are considered a vulnerable species. There is a great white shark research center in Cape Cod,Massachusetts dedicated to researching and protecting these magnificent creatures.

F

Made in United States
North Haven, CT
10 November 2022

26521074R00022